A Real Journey

Janie Price

A Real Journey

Janie Price

Beautiful
Books

First published 2011.

Beautiful Books Limited
36-38 Glasshouse Street
London W1B 5DL

www.beautiful-books.co.uk

ISBN 9781907616631

9 8 7 6 5 4 3 2 1

A catalogue reference for this book is available
from the British Library.

Cover design by Ian Pickard.
Typesetting by Misa Watanabe.
Printed in and bound in the UK by TJ International.

real (adj): 1. actually existing or occurring. 2. not artificial; genuine.

journey (noun): an act of travelling from one place to another.

reality TV (noun): a television programme in which real people are continuously filmed, designed to be entertaining rather than informative.

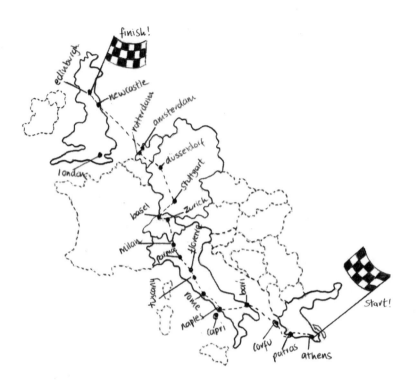

INTRODUCTION

Thursday 9ᵗʰ September, midnight
– Casperia, Lazio Region, Italy

The neighbourhood dogs are testing the natural acoustics of this southern Italian valley. It's midnight. Resistance is futile, but joining in isn't an option – I'm not fluent enough yet. Besides, barking in a shared remote village house just might get me evicted. Only one option I guess; I should start writing. After all, it's why I'm here.

I'm here because I'm not quite ready for my hometown, London. Too much has happened that needs to be recounted away from my natural surroundings. But this task is daunting. The screen I'm typing onto feels like a painter's canvas, and the problem with a blank canvas is that it's difficult to know where to put the first mark. So much space, so much potential, so much choice.

I am not a painter (although I do have a degree in art). I am not normally an author. I am a musician.

I started playing the cello when I was six years old and somehow, given many attempts to live life otherwise, I have spent the best part of my life in equal amounts trying, failing and, more recently, succeeding to make a living from my music.

I have also just experienced the most incredible, mad, brilliant five weeks of my life. So paint to canvas, bow to

1

string (metaphors notwithstanding), here I go…

On Monday 12th July, just under two months ago, I saw the advert on the internet. It was posted on a music jobs website, which until then, despite its best efforts, had failed to woo me with its offers.

This time, though, something caught my eye. Maybe it was me. Maybe I was longing for something a little more interesting than being in my flat in a failed relationship, the brittle strings of co-habitation seriously frayed from recent revelations of his chronic infidelity. Yes, certainly it was good timing.

A production company was looking for contributors for a new television series, titled *Art of Survival*. Stripped of cash, credit cards and help from friends, family and contacts, would it be possible to travel from Athens to Edinburgh in five weeks using only your artistic skill to survive? The whole process would be filmed and consequently televised for a six-part show for Sky Arts.

There would be a competitive element. Two artistic duos would be formed and required to compete to reach the final destination. Their earnings along the way would be logged and counted and whichever team made it to Edinburgh with the most money, including whatever was made on the final night – planned to coincide with the Edinburgh Festival – would win a cash prize of £5,000.

I updated my CV, glanced over at the man I had thought loved me who was preoccupied on his iPhone – presumably looking up the equation for the correct length of time for confessing infidelity divided by minutes spent looking vaguely remorseful multiplied by insane desire to leave the building – and decided it might be time to allow this job website to tempt me.

Apply for job. Auto-confirmation. Sent.

That's how I found myself in front of a panel of four people in a converted church hall in Waterloo being filmed with my cello, a loop unit I had never used before and a small battery-powered amp I had bought the day before in Copenhagen, where I had been playing a concert, from a man who should definitely consider starting a Danish ZZ Top Covers band. Despite the whiff of X Factor in the air with me facing a panel of five – three women, two men, thankfully none wearing trousers above their waist – I was pretty unfazed by the whole ordeal. And when the man who seemed to be in charge on the execution panel told me I wasn't what they were looking for, I was, quite frankly, as we say in south London, not bothered.

I took the opportunity to have a laugh with the people I was fairly convinced I would never see again, despite the inclusion of a camera-man filming the process, and as I packed up my gear and left, I had no feeling of real disappointment. At least I'd given it a try. In my line of work, if you can't roll with the punches, you are in the wrong job.

The breakdown of my relationship with 'the Ex' (as he shall be known for the purposes of this book) had left me a little nonplussed by life to say the least. You can imagine my surprise, then, when around mid-morning the next day (practically the only time I switch on a television, for my *Saturday Kitchen* watching hour) my mobile rang and the younger of the male producers I had met at the audition told me they had picked me for the show.

I'll be honest; it takes something of some gravity to tear me away from a demonstration on how to make good shortcrust pastry, but as the producer kept talking I realised it was actually a perfect time for me to leave my life in London. This was my chance to take on a new challenge. The time would have come soon anyway: the already frayed strings would snap in a month when the lease ran out on the flat I shared with the Ex, and negotiations on who would produce my next album would take at least another month. I had a couple of live music commitments, but nothing that couldn't be rearranged for after the five weeks I needed to be free to film the show.

And as it turned out, I would be leaving sooner rather than later. A lot sooner, in fact, said the producer. In six days.

PREPARATION

I am sad. I see our days are numbered. We have been through many adventures together, and one of us has even been dropped down a toilet, but still he rings faithfully. But I'm afraid, my old friend Nokia, it is time for us to part. With a curious resemblance to the treatment I have recently received from the Ex, I will be trading this one in for a newer, younger model. I think I am probably the least likely traditionalist in the world, but when it comes to mobile phones I have never understood the need for technological progression. Predictive texting invariably means in a hurry you end up telling someone 'meat mr at eight for barred dranks with moon' or worse, you manage a grammatically perfect message only to receive back 'lol nice2cu cl sn'. Urm…?! Phones with cameras (that always take substandard pictures); phones with a compass (what happens when the battery dies and you're halfway across the Sahara, presuming of course you have a signal to start with); phones with stop watches… Please can I just make a bloody call – you know, like in the good old days?

But, not forgetting the adventure I am about to undertake is also a competition, there are some rules I have to adhere to. There are many things I am not allowed, but I am permitted a few small perks. One of these is a mobile phone which I can use throughout the trip, but not to further my progress in the competition in any way. I realise the one thing I want to be able to do is update my friends and family on at least the vague details of my journey that the show allows, as well as the small (but perfectly formed) fan-base I have as a recording artist. I also thought that this one-way communication could become a small incentive for me to keep going on the tougher days I presumed would inevitably occur with no money and no guarantees I would make enough to survive.

I would need the internet; I would need an iPhone.

I feel guilty, Nokia is in pieces. (I had to deconstruct it to retrieve my Sim card.) I sit here unpeeling the packaging of my latest squeeze layer by unenvironmentally-friendly layer, until ah, there it is, sleek and shiny and momentarily I feel excited by my acquisition, until I realise I have no idea how it works. By some cruel twist of fate the phone has been imported from Italy (homeland of the Ex) with a manual I can only hope to vaguely understand. It may take the next five weeks just to work out how to switch the damn thing on...

Of course, this was not the only thing I had to sort out before walking out of my current home and taking a flight to meet a complete stranger in a square in Athens, accompanied by an equally unfamiliar group of people known to me only at this point in time as the producer and his TV crew. I single-handedly – the Ex had since retreated to his homeland – moved as much as I could out of the flat to my long-suffering parents' spare room. I rearranged commitments and made a list of practical essentials I would need to pack: torch, emergency battery charger, sleeping bag, chewing gum, at least three pairs of sunglasses.

The six days preceding departure were madness. And talking of which, I also had things the show required me to do – such as see a psychiatrist. This was particularly weird for me. My mother had suffered a bout of depression when I was a teenager, which affected me quite deeply at the time. It had been so bad she had consequently been hospitalised for a while and I had suffered awful panic attacks – a sort of sympathy sickness – the ghosts of which had hung around throughout my early twenties. I was nervous. But this was a good feeling in a way, as it made me realise how much taking this challenge meant to me and how much I didn't want to be told I was unable to go. I was also comforted by the fact the production company were responsible enough to make sure none of the contributors (as we were apparently to be called) were raving nutters; it bode well for the potential of having a good team-mate.

As it happened, I had little to worry about. Mary, the hired psychiatrist, was a lovely women who, after establishing I did not hear voices in my head (at least not of the demonic type she was inferring), nor suffer from any other mental instability that might make me an unsuitable candidate for the show – I'm guessing agoraphobia could be a problem and schizophrenia might be unsettling for a team-mate – pronounced I was in a perfectly good mental state to take on the proposed challenge. My father later took great delight in telling me she'd definitely got that one wrong: I must be completely insane to undertake such an adventure. I have to admit, I agreed with him.

The final challenge before I set off was what the production company called an 'at-home shoot'. Two days before departure, there was a knock on the door of my semi-naked flat (only the Ex's belongings and that which I needed for last minute music work and travelling remained). Upon opening, I was met by one very large camera with what I could only presume in the darkness of the hallway to be a human behind it. Suddenly reality or, to be precise, reality TV, hit me.

It seems ridiculous to say, but it was the one aspect of the challenge I had not prepared myself for. Rarely watching television (Saturday treat aside), I had little regard for its cultural dominance and even less of a yearning to be part of its process, and so the opportunity to be filmed had definitely not played a major part in my deciding to apply for the show. Consciously, it had been the lure of an adventure I would probably otherwise never be given the opportunity to have in my lifetime, combining my two first loves, music and travelling.

But here I was, with a man (or a woman with incredibly hairy legs) with a very big camera connected by a thick black lead to another man holding a huge boom mike, followed by a man I recognised as the younger producer from the execution panel, and Stef, a short, elfin-like, beautiful, dark-haired girl I would later come to know as the AP, or assistant producer for those of you who know as little about TV production as I did.

Furniture was moved around and items I was packing were laid out in a more eye-pleasing composition on the bed I had not been able to sleep in since the Ex had left. Not that I had slept much on the living room sofa since preparing for the show. Each night I was gripped by a new score in the game of fear versus excitement – normally it was 2-1 to the former.

Strangely, and completely unpredictably bearing in mind my lack of experience, I had not felt nervous in front of the camera. Previously I had performed on TV both as a session musician and promoting my own albums playing selected songs, but never really talking to camera as it became evident I would be expected to do daily as part of the journey. I decided instantly that I would treat it in the same way I did an audience when I was performing as a musician. It would become my friend, and I would imagine the rest of my friends, sitting in miniature behind the inky blackness of the lens, and would pretend I was talking to them. I just hoped they didn't mind me turning them into some sort of mind-eyed extras for Gulliver's travels in order for me to get through this.

I learnt quickly: 'Don't look straight into the camera, look at the producer', who would be standing next to the camera-man. And also, 'Don't wear stripes or red'. I found to my surprise and relief I quite enjoyed being filmed and was rewarded with compliments that I was 'a natural', but I couldn't help thinking they probably said that to all the contributors two days before flying them off to begin a seemingly almost impossible challenge, which only the – apparently not clinically – insane would attempt.

I also realised that these four people, plus the unknown team-mate whom I was told on camera that day was a "visual artist" and male, would become my travelling companions for the next five weeks. It was all slightly overwhelming. The producer had written the idea for the show, and although he had been charmingly self-deprecating on the phone, 'the bad news is you've got me...(*little chuckle, audible 'trust me' smile*),' I didn't buy it for a minute. He was smart. The crew left in the same whirl of energy in which they arrived. I had shot my first ever reality TV 'piece to camera'. I was fairly sure I hadn't said anything ridiculous. Great – but I'd have to do this for another 36 days! I realised I was shaking a little from the adrenalin. I opened a beer and decided which pair of sunglasses would have to forgo the adventure.

THE DAY BEFORE

I am not prone to consciously acknowledging monumental life moments, generally due to the fact that it is fairly true of human nature that you only realise their gravity after they are over, but on the last morning I woke up in my flat, I felt an overwhelming sense of finality. I would never wake up here again. I could not recall any time in my life when I had taken on a challenge this great, a change so definite and a future so uncertain.

Curiously, I felt quite numb. I'm sure Mary would have had a fascinating explanation for this – probably to do with coping strategies – but all I could think about was concern that the excitement had left and a mild but distant fear somewhere in the pit of my stomach had replaced it. I suppose it could also have just been last night's takeaway with my friends, 'the last supper' repeating, but I was pretty sure that wasn't it.

I dragged the last of my packed boxes past the recently-moved-in neighbours' flat and downstairs to my best friend's car, which she'd lent me for the day. I could hear laughing behind their newly-acquired front door and the smell of fresh paint, and I felt unbelievably sad to be leaving and yet unbelievably ready to start redecorating my own little house of me, which I suddenly realised hadn't had a fresh coat of paint for some time. Either the takeaway had suddenly digested or I was getting excited again. Bring it on, Athens...

DEPARTURE

Friday 30th July, 3.48am

I am still unable to sleep, and now fear is the overriding emotion again. I am panic drinking instant hot chocolate (three down, one sachet to go). Night-time TV offers absolutely no comfort given the fact I am about to become one of its subjects – and that at 4am there is an apparent choice of, well, nothing to watch. I start to think about the journey. The very nature of it is such that I have absolutely no way of knowing what will happen, and so prediction would be completely nonsensical. I turn instead to what I might like to get personally out of it. I decide, given my current, sugar-fuelled, wide-eyed, wired state, that it would be nice if I was less fearful of the unknown. And maybe a little less addicted to late-night hot chocolate.

I also realise that I feel woefully under-prepared for this trip in terms of luggage. I am using new equipment that I have not had time to practise with properly. I was asked to use only equipment that could be powered by battery as they expected me to be playing mainly outside in locations that might not have access to electricity, and this has meant sourcing a loop unit and amp that I already suspect will be insufficient for my needs.

Two years ago I recorded my album *Girl and a Cello*. It was my second record and I wanted to try something a bit different from my first, which was very much a band driven singer/songwriter accomplishment. As cello is my main instrument, I wanted to make it more of a feature and, spurred on by a suggestion from my record producer and crazy Icelandic friend, I decided to attempt recording the entire album using only my cello and voice. The idea was simple; to create pop songs in the way I normally wrote them, but with the help of studio equipment and it's tricks, and to use the cello to create the other instruments that would usually feature in these songs.

So, for example, the drums were created by playing with jazz drum brushes on the back of the cello body. I even kicked it, with a soft shoe, of course, to create a good kick-drum sound. We pitch shifted (put into a lower scale range) the cello down to create bass lines and put it through effects to create sounds closer to a guitar. Everything else I did with voice, cymbals (I'm now an expert at orally recreating a drum-kit hi hat sound), atmospheric sounds etc.

Working with such limitations – I promise I didn't cheat, even though I was tempted a few times – was refreshing for me as a musician and I was very happy with the outcome. However, it did pose a big problem – how could I recreate this live? Obviously, using a band seemed ridiculous. I wanted people to understand the concept and to represent the recording honestly, live. After some investigation I decided upon using a loop unit with the cello. This unit, which the cello plugs into via a small amplification device and input placed on the cello body, allows me to record and loop tracks of cello and/or voice. This means I am able to build up tracks of sounds to create chords and percussion over which I can sing the song. The unit is a beast with three pedals so I can switch between recorded tracks, working verses and choruses.

Only one problem: the unit is so powerful it will not work with batteries. It needs an external power supply and so will be impossible to take on this journey. I found a much smaller version of the unit that could be used with batteries, but of course this gives less freedom for interchanging tracks, since it has only one pedal. The other problem is amplification. Normally I have the luxury of performing in venues with PA systems and sound engineers to help me, now all I would have to rely on would be a small battery powered amp. This will be an entirely new challenge for me if I am to play the type of music I specialise in and not default to classical music, in which I am neither well-rehearsed or – after years away from my classical training – confident in playing.

And yet, in spite of this, I can feel somewhere a bead of yesterday's excitement.

Katie Price, aka Jordan, is currently gracing the early morning television screen. An advert for a show enticingly titled *What Katie Did Next* has just stirred me from my sugar-fuelled stupor and I realise I have absolutely nothing to fear – if that much plastic can venture into a jungle without melting, I'm definitely in with a chance.

In the end I do not sleep at all, but settle into the fact that while slumber eludes me adventure awaits me.

The cab I've booked turns up punctually and, for the first time, I carry everything I have packed for the trip. It weighs a ton, well, perhaps not quite a ton, more like 25-30kg. Comprising a rucksack containing all my electrical music gear (loop unit, amp and leads), the cello in its fibre-glass wheelie case and a suitcase with my clothes and essentials, which I decide is a good practical move as I can sit on it in lieu of a seat, which is a fairly essential item for a cellist.

I currently weigh 52kg. I suddenly have an inordinate amount of respect for ants that can carry ten or more times their own body weight. Humbled by this fact, I stumble outside to meet my cab driver with whom I spend the journey to the airport chatting, consequently thrilled by the idea of my adventure and get excited about it all over again. I arrive at Gatwick, along with my new-found enthusiasm, and celebrate by buying another pair of sunglasses for the trip.

I receive a text from the producer while I'm negotiating eating my early morning airside vendor breakfast with a plastic knife and fork. (I'm all for airport security but when I could go to the duty-free shop next door and buy highly flammable spirit in an easily breakable solid glass bottle, I'm at a slight loss as to why I'm not trusted with real cutlery.) My team-mate is taking the same flight and, should we meet, can we try not to talk to each other?

Naturally, I therefore spend the entire time I am waiting for the flight – a good two hours as I am always stupidly early for catching any mode of transport, I hate the stress of rushing – searching the crowds for my potential team-mate. This results in some seriously unwanted attention from 'arty looking' types, but since I have held an inappropriate amount of eye contact with them, it is entirely my own fault.

As it happens, despite the glaringly obvious clue of a cello strapped into the seat next to me, I do not bump into my team-mate. On arrival in Athens, I have the ridiculous good fortune of my baggage arriving almost instantly (must be a good omen, I decide) and walk out to a man with a sign bearing my name. Half an hour later I pull up at a very swanky hotel in the centre of Athens and am greeted by the producer, who ushers me in gingerly, presumably aware my team-mate must be in a cab right behind me.

I find myself in a beautiful room that I am only allowed out of during the first half of every hour. My team-mate-to-be apparently gets the second half to experience freedom from the constraints of a walk-in shower and on-tap room service menu. I can't see what they are worrying about. Presented with such a set-up, most artists I know wouldn't think of straying outside of the room, particularly when the mini bar is paid for.

I make the uncharacteristically sensible selection of a Diet Coke from the little fridge, switch on the TV, and spend a bizarre yet weirdly delightful half-an-hour watching what I can only suppose to be the Greek version of *Eastenders*. The opening credits show various members of a family hitting each other over the head with pans and jumping out of what look to me like giant wine kegs, accompanied by music I can only assume was written by the same composer who worked on early episodes of *Benny Hill*.

But despite the lure of Greek soap opera, I can hear Athens outside and I know a little escape during my allotted half-an-hour is in order.

I meet a few locals. One man, while walking down the street behind me, tries his very best chat-up line;

guessing – I suppose from the blonde hair and blue eyes – that I am probably not a Greek national, he manages in English, 'Follow me, lovely.' Now, I have to tell you that while I was flattered (despite the omission of two front teeth from his oral equation), I recalled a lecture at school many years ago about going off with strangers and decided that this was a time to heed it – and, besides, I only have 20 minutes left, not nearly enough time to see either his 'etchings' or 'stamp collection'. So after a quick trip into a local bakery to get a drink, and mentally noting just how different Diet Coke tastes in other countries, I retreat to the safety of the hotel. Here I finally manage to fall asleep, until the camera-man and sound-man call me to tell me they will be taking me for dinner tonight on the hotel roof terrace. Stef and the producer will be taking the as yet unknown team-mate to another location.

It's a beautiful night and the view is amazing overlooking the Acropolis. It feels unreal. We laugh a lot and I feel relieved that we are having fun – I hope this sets the tone for the coming weeks. Then the producer turns up: I am to go to bed. I think he is joking; he is not. He has things to tell the crew that I am not allowed to know. Reality kicks in, I am part of a game I do not fully understand the rules of. I suddenly wish dearly that I had read the quick setup guide before ripping open all the packaging and trying to play. What am I doing here?

I remember shaking my head in disbelief during an unfortunate remote control flicking incident where I once accidently happened upon *Big Brother*. Curiosity compelled me to listen for ten minutes to a room full of people talking about virtually nothing; one was clipping their toenails, another discussing the merits of brown rice over white. I truly couldn't understand why these people wanted the world to watch them, and nor could I understand why a large percentage of the world wanted to do so.

So why am I participating in a reality TV show? I realise the only way to gain clarity is to stay and find out.

Saturday 31st July – DAY 1
– ATHENS

I feel a little bit like a pig being fed up for market (or at least how I imagine one to feel). The producer meets me alone for my five-star breakfast experience at the set time he had dictated the night before and explains the schedule for the day.

Back in my room, which I must now stay in until filming starts this afternoon, I wonder about my team-mate. I wonder why he applied for the show, and what and whom he might be leaving behind in England. Would we become friends? Share likes, dislikes, have anything other than both being participants in the show in common? Safe in the knowledge I would soon be finding out, I decide to take a last sorely needed chance to practise with my new equipment.

I set up a little amplified practice studio in my hotel room. Playing goes well, despite this being a new way of working for me. It's comforting to be playing my cello in these unfamiliar surroundings and I feel optimistic that as long as I have music everything will be ok; it has been and always will be the one constant in my life.

I spread the map of Europe that I bought last week out onto the bed and look at the options we have for journeying to Edinburgh from Athens, which seems like a ludicrously long way right now. The producer has already warned me that there are some places north of Greece on this side of the Adriatic that will be difficult, in fact impossible, to travel through with the camera and crew. There are possible ways to travel through most of eastern Europe, but I make a quick decision, given the chance that some routes may be restricted, that it would make sense to travel from Greece to Italy, across western Europe. I was also taking into account my only previous experience of eastern Europe, which had been a backpacking adventure with a classmate when I was at art college. We decided to celebrate her birthday with a trip to Serbia, lured by the promise of a music festival and the possibility of visiting neighbouring countries Hungary and Croatia cheaply by train. During one particularly memorable portion of the journey we spent fifteen hours on a train which had to stop at regular intervals so the train crew could spend a worryingly large amount of time outside the stationary vehicle banging it with what sounded like large hammers, until eventually our museum-worthy mode of transport would creak and jolt back into slow motion.

It had still been a fantastic journey, and the people

we met had been incredibly friendly despite frequent language barriers, in addition (a great plus for poor art students) the food and drink were very inexpensive. But taking into account the pros and cons, the fact remains that I'm more familiar with travelling in western European countries and, aware that I may be pandering to my own need to seek comfort in reliable chartered territory over something more unpredictable (which I feel this challenge has enough potential for regardless of which route is chosen), my eyes gravitate excitedly to the dotted routes on the map indicating possible travel from a Greek port called Igoumentisa to Brindisi or Bari in Italy. But I haven't met my team-mate yet – maybe he will have different ideas.

Sunday 1st August, 12.40am

I am finally sitting down. I am exhausted but also elated. I have made it through the first day, not homeless, nor starving. My first 'home' is a small, simple, clean hotel at the foothills of the Acropolis. It's not five star, but it's also not too shabby considering I was fully prepared to sleep under an Athenian olive tree tonight.

The producer came to collect me from my luxury makeshift rehearsal space/hotel room at 2pm and the gravity of what I was about to attempt hit me immediately as I struggled down the uneven Athens roads with all my gear in the thirty-eight degree heat. Broken, aching and sweating, I realised I'd only actually been walking for five minutes.

However, nervous excitement surpassed any real feelings of discomfort and provided enough adrenalin to power me towards a little café next to a beautiful old square in the centre of town, where I was given a Diet Coke along with instructions to wait for the crew to come. From there we would walk together back up to the square where I would finally, on camera, meet the person who would become my close travelling companion and fellow survivee for the next five weeks. I can't recall any other time in my life when I have truly felt such an overwhelming mix of emotions. How can you prepare yourself for an experience you have no previous knowledge of? Well, the answer is, of course, that you cannot, so you drink your fizzy drink too quickly, spend five minutes trying to extract the trapped carbon dioxide from somewhere deep in your ribcage, which waits until precisely the moment you wish it had stayed where it was. 'Nice to meet you,' I half say, but mainly burp out, on camera to my new team-mate and, quickly surmising from the luggage he has surrounding him, painter, Johan. He smiles, we shake hands – team JJ, as we will become known, has officially formed.

I make some quick observations. Johan is younger (ten years my junior), smaller (a thin boyish frame) and darker than I expected. I'd found out in advance he was called Johan and had expected a blond Scandinavian; he is in fact half Swedish and half Sri-Lankan, a genetic mix providing him with looks that I'm ashamed to admit I hope prove useful in engaging the sympathy and consequent help of the odd young lady or two during our trip. I don't have time for further evaluation, as the producer is handing us an envelope which, after some polite and quite frankly very English, 'no you open it's, I proceed to tear open.

It contains the pictures of two girls and two CVs. Initially I am surprised – what is this? I had been sure both teams would be mixed boy and girl, mainly from a practical point of view as I thought it would be slightly safer (call me old-fashioned) to be with a man in the eventuality that we would have to sleep rough or hitchhike. Consequently, it took a good couple of seconds before I realised that it was in fact the identity of our opposition that was being revealed to us.

I was only mildly surprised to find myself for the most part uninterested in the information. I had my own journey to make and a guy standing next to me, with whom I had yet to speak more than two complete sentences, who would be taking it with me. Quite frankly, that was enough for me to be dealing with. However, despite the fact that the television show also being a competition had never been a motivation for my taking part, curiosity, and the fact a camera was filming my every move and reaction, did ensure I looked for long enough to see we were up against an opera singer and a classical cellist. Cue chill up my spine (no mean feat in a southern Grecian city in July). My worst fear confirmed.

Although I trained classically as a cellist, as a teenager I decided to leave the world of black evening dresses, freezing cold Christmas concerts in churches, which necessitated wearing woolly gloves until the moment right before performing, and hairy conductors with cummerbunds. I found the snobbery and lack of freedom I had felt as a young classical musician completely suffocating and took the first opportunity I could to exercise my skills in an alternative environment.

I jammed in pubs and clubs with anyone who'd let me. Early forays included attempting to play in a plastic mini skirt in a punk bar in Camden and an almost identical skirt (apparently I had learnt nothing about how difficult this was with a cello the first time around) with several rock bands. I was about twenty when I got my first lucky break and a taste of how it could be to earn a living using my music, something I had truly not considered a realistic possibility after meeting the careers adviser at high school. I remember her weeping at my musical aspirations; I think she used to be a professional pianist.

I had just returned from almost a year working on a camp-site in south-west France, where I had spent my time cleaning tents, running the kids' club, learning French and rotting chunks of my young stomach lining with the cheapest local wine (before the days of EU directives, I am pretty sure it would now be called vinegar). Although I had passed my GSCEs and A-levels well, I hadn't wanted to go to university, but still wasn't sure what it was I did want to do. I hadn't been able to hear the careers adviser's suggestions between her gulps and sniffs. So, France was my sort of gap year, but it didn't provide me with any insight into a possible future career (just a mild digestive problem for a year or so afterwards).

But when I came back to the UK I met a bass player

in a London-based band, who suggested I should try and work as a musician. And, by chance, I found a recording studio nearby in Fulham, South London, which was looking for a kitchen assistant/human dish washer. Ok, I wasn't playing the cello in there but at least I would be in the right environment to find a way to do so.

It proved to be the right move. My break came when, after telling everyone who worked there that I played the cello, a cellist was required for a recording session. They were skeptical, but I was there, the need was urgent, and I did wash the dishes particularly well so maybe I might be ok on the cello. Apparently I was, and the producer was so pleased he recommended me to a session agency. Cue my foray into a new world I hadn't even considered being able to work in previously. In stark contrast to the classical world I had known, here was an environment in which I was actively encouraged to display my passion for music. Swaying with a cello while playing was definitely allowed, the more rock and roll the better. Quirky style with regard to outfit choice was almost a must and I would also be paid to be actively creative. Writing new cello lines for pop, rock and dance songs – making my sound blend and enhance many other genres of music. I had found a home for my skills.

However, throughout the ensuing years, I never quite managed to shake off the ghost of classical past and the feeling that in choosing not to complete my classical training – I didn't take my grades after passing 5, although I subsequently played to a much higher standard – I was somehow a lesser musician. Of course, from a rational point of view, my musical accomplishments would prove this insecurity unfounded, but self-doubt is still a very real and often destructive feeling. As I felt it surface on seeing my competitors' CVs, I knew I urgently needed to find a way to conquer this feeling, and an almost instant sense of relief in realising I could do so because I had to.

I had just discovered at least one of the purposes of this journey for me. The importance of recognising and dealing with feelings of self-doubt, and finding a way to turn them into useful, positive, practical feelings with which I might achieve things I had not previously thought I could. It might seem ridiculously obvious, but as adults it is rare we give ourselves the opportunity to challenge deep-rooted feelings and long-held beliefs in this way.

I passed the envelope back to the producer and decided it was time to have a go at earning some money. Thirty-eight degree heat makes a girl thirsty and for the first time in my life I was unable to buy a bottle of water when I needed it.

I set up my little amp and loop unit in the middle of the square and sat down on a wall that felt a bit like, I can only imagine, putting your bottom on a lit barbecue grill. Sweating, thirsty and overwhelmed by the enormity of what I suddenly realised I had undertaken, a well-done pair of bottom cheeks were the least of my worries – the fact that the little travel amp which had performed so well indoors did not carry sound at all outdoors was a much bigger problem.

I had to make a quick decision: sit here failing on film five minutes into the challenge or default to playing some classical tunes acoustically. Cue second chill up spine... I hadn't played classical music for years. And though I'd brought easy sheet music as an emergency back up, I wasn't expecting an emergency quite so early on in the proceedings. I suddenly realised I was massively out of my depth and being filmed trying metaphorically not to sink.

Unlikely salvation came in the form of a group of drunken English-speaking tourists who slung notes into my cello case. Normally, as a person who enjoys travelling, I am mortified by the behavior of a shamefully large proportion of my fellow countrymen and (increasingly) women abroad. It entirely baffles me why anyone would make the effort to pack a suitcase and embark on a journey often requiring many hours of travelling, only to completely ignore their new, exciting, culturally different surroundings, hotfoot it to the nearest Irish bar (of which, curiously, there seems to be one in every single city in the world) and seek out the nearest food outlet selling 'breakfast like Mum makes it' – and then to complain that the beans don't taste quite like the ones at home.

But on this occasion I found myself shamefully delighted by this slobbering, stumbling group and very grateful for their obliterated state. They didn't care; the exchange rate was favourable and try as they might, and indeed it looked like they had been trying very, very hard, they couldn't spend all the 'funny money' in their pockets on Guinness and fried breakfasts, so there was some left over for the mad girl melting in the heat playing something they'd heard on a car advert. I thanked them profusely – bad move, they wanted to join in with the singing. And join in they did, on camera. I found myself wondering how many times I might find myself in situations I would normally find uncomfortable which, due to the nature of needing to survive, I would have to embrace. I worried how far I might let this go, how many values I might compromise and, even worse, be filmed doing so.

Johan meanwhile had also abandoned his plan of painting on a large canvas and was instead using a pad to sketch people's portraits in the (much more sensible choice of) shade. He had met an American mother and daughter from San Francisco and was doing a portrait of the daughter. He had negotiated a special half-price rate in exchange for the opportunity to take a swim in the pool of their 'just round the corner', luxury hotel.

Alarm bells instantly rang in my head. We were less than two hours into this challenge and Johan was intending, effectively, to spend a potentially precious twenty euros on a dip in a pool. I decided to ignore the bells – Mary might be watching – and maybe it was a good idea; we were hot, I was not enjoying my outdoor classical performance to camera at all and we still had all evening to earn enough for a room for the night. Not to mention the fact we were supposed to be having an adventure, and maybe this was Johan's way of embracing it. It was certainly too early on for me to be the one to make a call that might thwart his enthusiasm.

The hotel pool proved to be neither just round the corner nor available for non-hotel guests, particularly those so unable to blend with the paying clientele, due to the fact we were a) dressed like travellers with massive rucksacks b) carrying a sizable instrument and a huge roll of canvas and c) being followed by a four man/woman TV crew.

Exhausted and slightly frustrated, small knots of worry started to form in my stomach, matching those that had formed across my shoulders and back as I tried to keep up with Johan and the two American human gazelles. I had never seen a sixty-something-year-old San Franciscan woman walk so fast. Was my team-mate always going to be swayed so easily by the promises of treats from strangers? (Thank goodness he hadn't met the man outside the bakery yesterday.) I had a sudden flash of memory from the 1968 film *Chitty Chitty Bang Bang*, where the child-catcher ensnares the two Arian-looking children with promises of candy and them traps them in a cage in a travelling caravan…I decide the only way to deal with the situation is to take control.

Narrowly escaping the embarrassment of being forcibly evicted from one of the most expensive hotels in Athens with a timely voluntary exit, I learn the first important lesson of the trip. Never, ever try and use a revolving door, no matter how large it appears to be, when you are carrying two bags and a cello.

We step back out into the glare of the late afternoon Athens sun, limbs miraculously intact, and I spy a taxi rank.

My Dad is a taxi driver, a licensed black taxi driver aka 'London Cabbie', a fact I take constant delight in sharing with other cabbies I meet taking taxis in London. Cue swapping of stories and lifelong friendship by the end of the journey, no matter how long or short. I have discovered, too, that the London cabbie really is a unique breed. This is not just my biased opinion – here are some facts.

There are 21,000 drivers currently licensed in London and all of them, despite the invention of the GPS satellite navigation system, still have to pass an exam known as 'the Knowledge', which was introduced in 1865 and hasn't changed much since. It takes an average of thirty-four months to prepare for the exam, and they learn the streets of London in a way that turns them into human A-Zs. I'm sure this makes them the world's most informed drivers relative to their city, but I'm also ever hopeful of finding a similarly well-informed cheekie chappie behind the wheel of the London taxi's international counterparts. Sadly, in my experience, this is not often the case.

There's New York, where the driver has no idea where anything is but will still pretend he or she does for an inordinate amount of time, at your cost. And Bangkok where a ride in a tuk tuk once involved me literally hanging on for dear life as I sat encased in a small, three-wheeled auto-rickshaw decorated in birthday wrapping paper and multi-coloured lights, chauffeured by the Thai version of Michael Schumacher who made an interesting and unscheduled stop at a tailors I had no inclination to visit, but which the driver insisted upon as he was given petrol vouchers for everyone he introduced to his friend's emporium of bad taste. I politely wandered around for ten minutes before resuming the planned trip back to my hotel at breakneck speed.

Despite this, I remain optimistic. We need help now and maybe the Greek cab drivers will offer salvation.

As it happens, one does. After five minutes of gesticulation and the kind of shouty, pidgin English I am normally embarrassed to witness fellow Brits practising abroad, a sweet, old Greek driver nods and smiles and offers to take us, and then promptly disappears.

Maybe my frantic arm movements had scared him? Apparently not, as he returns ten minutes later (we have not moved, unsure of what to do next we had remained static) and offers to take us for free to a spot more suitable for two busking artists.

He patiently crams Johan and me, our camera-man, plus all our belongings, into his small taxi. As it turns out, our road angel speaks enough English to give us a short précis of his philosophy of life. He tells us that we in northern Europe have it wrong. We live too fast and we don't enjoy the simple pleasures of love, family, of being alive. I have to say, I was in total agreement and was instantly reminded why I was there, with the lens of a camera digging into my ribs and the nervous knee shake of a pool-loving painter to my left: I needed to reconnect with the world and remember a few basic truths.

Destination of the Acropolis hill reached, we bade our chauffeur/philosopher a fond farewell, and promptly realised we had a lot of competition. It was as if we had stepped into an international outdoor busking convention. Artistic entrepreneurs of all shapes, sizes and disciplines, stood metres apart, lining the route up the hill. I have never seen such a display of woolen scarves, berets and spectacles (and that was just from the man on my left). All of them had perfect little set-ups, the musicians with neat wheelie trolleys housing perfectly functioning amps; the artists with utility belts housing paints and brushes and portable easels. We were definitely out of our league here.

But then something pleasantly unexpected happened: Johan took charge. He walked into a little restaurant halfway down the hill. By this time we were starving, we'd had nothing to eat since our first meeting in the square and only a bottle of water between us. In exchange for a portrait and a short performance from me, he negotiated food for us, which soon appeared in the form of two little warm foil trays.

Technically, the meatballs that consequently greeted us were the worst I had ever eaten (I was at school the last time and the benchmark was therefore set pretty low), but they still tasted amazing to us, because we had earned them and because we needed them. Up until this point, I hadn't even eaten meat for years – purely a taste choice, I own leather bags and shoes so can't profess to being a staunch vegetarian. I had fully prepared myself for the eventuality that a challenge this great would at times demand not only mental but also physical compromise, and here was the first of the latter. Having just a moment ago felt nauseous and faint, we were now bolstered solely by the generosity of complete strangers.

What's more, on hearing our story, the restaurant owners had an idea: they had another place, a roof terrace restaurant upstairs, where I could do a little concert. We could take a hat around the tables and see if we could earn some money.

Upstairs, the crew promptly chose a table and ordered a feast the Greek God Zeus would have been proud of (not a meatball in sight). I was a little surprised, however, that I didn't feel any resentment towards the crew considering the comparative luxury they were experiencing. I realise they have chosen a job, not a challenge in the way Johan and I have. Why should they suffer and not eat properly as they would on any other filming project? I also have to credit my feeling in part to their handling of the situation. If anything they seemed very aware of the stark contrast between us as contributors and them as paid crew and a little awkward to be dining so handsomely in front of us, especially as just the night before we had been eating together, equally, in a five star hotel restaurant. I wonder how this dynamic between Johan and me and them will play out as the journey continues. Will we ever be able to afford to eat with them? Will they feel tempted to help us somehow (although the rules of the programme forbid this)? Will we be tempted to accept forbidden help if it's offered and we are starving?

I found a space in the middle of the terrace, surrounded by eager diners in the mid-evening heat, which had subsided only to the point that I was no longer melting, just gently roasting. Lit by candles and the excess light flooding from the Acropolis at the top of the hill, and with small beads of involuntary dribble escaping my mouth as a relentless flow of waiters passed in front of me carrying trays of Greek delicacies, I began to play a few pieces from the classical books I had brought with me.

Halfway through, I stood up and addressed the packed terrace. I explained our challenge to the obvious amusement (or maybe bemusement) of the diners whose tables Johan consequently visited with my hat while I continued to play. It's interesting that we are allowed to explain the challenge. I wonder how it would be if we were not. I have never known of a busker explaining their story before playing, but then I've also never seen one being trailed by a film crew. Somehow we managed to make eighty-four euros. We were saved. This would be enough for a room for us each somewhere cheap if we added it to the rest of the money we had made in the square, sixty-seven euros. We celebrated with a half of lager each, on the house.

Propped up by the small terrace bar, Johan promptly struck up conversation with two Canadians, hoping to get a portrait commission, which he did. They were an interesting duo. They were both travelling alone and had met in Athens. On striking up conversation they discovered they were not only from the same country, but had studied at the same institution in the same town. Tonight they were celebrating this amazing coincidence and would continue to do so later at a James Bond-themed party they had heard about.

Johan wanted to go. Apprehensive after the swimming pool debacle earlier, I wasn't keen to follow another set of strangers to a place which would clearly be of no use in furthering our journey, and besides, I had nothing to wear. I did have the fleeting idea of either painting a digit and going as Goldfinger, or maybe Johan and I could recreate the cello case scene in *The*

Living Daylights and glide down the Acropolis hillside using the case? Luckily for me, on overhearing Johan's proposed spy-themed jaunt, the producer put an end to these plans immediately. No way, it was only day one and we would need to be fresh for the morning.

The restaurant owner turns out to be a wonderful man and incredibly helpful. He makes suggestions for possible routes out of Athens, saying it could be a good idea to head to the south-western port of Patras, from there we can catch a boat and travel north. He also recommends a cheap hotel nearby. I think I have misheard him when he says the name and ask him to write it down. No, I have not, we are going to ask for a room at Hotel Erecthion. Stifling school girl giggles – and hoping it means something else in Greek and that the lighting in the rooms is not provided by red bulbs – we make our way to our first night's shelter. I realise I am comforted by the thought that, despite the dubious name of our hotel, at least I have not yet knowingly sworn on camera. Mum would be proud.

The hotel actually turns out to be much less sleazy then any English pronunciation of its name might lead one to suspect. My room is a large double, favouring a 'beige theme', with a small shower and toilet. I even have a little balcony. It's definitely not comparable to last night's luxury, but considering the other possibilities had we not made any money today, I don't feel any need to call down to reception and ask why the TV doesn't work and there's a black sock in the shower.

Sunday 1st August DAY 2:
– ATHENS TO PATRAS

The next morning I wake up to the sounds of the Sunday church bells next door playing an unfamiliar combination of notes that make pleasing, unfamiliar scales. It's already very hot and I can hear someone hosing their garden, or maybe their own overheated flesh. Watching the tangle of electricity lines weaving their way across my view of the Acropolis, I'm aware of a very definite pain in my back. It doesn't worry me, I'll toughen up. I have to.

In the small but perfectly formed breakfast room of 'Hotel Male Arousal' (which, I'm relieved to say, I saw no evidence of last night), I'm greeted by fresh Greek coffee and hot bread and jam, but no Johan. It would appear he's not an early morning person. However, I do meet the crew, who are clearly rattled. The production car has been broken into. If I'm absolutely honest, I'm not surprised. A huge, brand new black Range Rover is not the most inconspicuous vehicle to be driving through southern Europe. Maybe leaving it in a quiet side street in one of the most cash-strapped cities in the European community was not such a good idea. The camera-man had suffered most with almost all of his gear stolen, but at least all the essential filming equipment had been stored in the hotel rooms.

Nervous excitement returns (or maybe it's the Greek coffee kicking in). Where would we go next? In a weird way I'm ready to move on. Although we are only on day two of the challenge, I feel like we have been through so much already, and it also feels like it's time to put some kilometres between us and the first destination. Johan and I manage to secure our next free taxi ride from a man who looks like he would be better suited to being in a famous rock band or driving a large Range Rover with a busted, taped-up window. He brings us to the main bus station where we hope, following the advice of last night's restauranteur, to take a coach to the port of Patras accompanied by the producer, camera-man and sound-man.

We don't have enough money for the ticket when we arrive (bearing in mind we will also need to get boat tickets at the port) but Johan quickly secures a portrait commission from an American man for his son. I set up next to him and play. I am soon joined by an old man with a melodica, and while I don't earn us any money I do spend a magical ten minutes jamming with this stranger.

The American proves to be generous and pays enough for us to get our coach, and so we set off on a two-and-a-half-hour journey along a beautiful southern coastal road. The drive gives me time to reflect on an incident at the coach station earlier. As we were queuing to board, a couple got very agitated by the camera. It wasn't even filming at that time, but they weren't aware of this. After initial shouting and much gesticulation in lieu of mutually understandable words, the situation was quickly resolved, but their reaction had shocked me. I realised there would possibly be moments when the camera would actually be a hindrance for us and potentially offensive to people. I totally understood. Cameras are inherently invasive and the fact that, given this piece of machinery, people feel able to stare, point and record the lives of others who do not always volunteer to be filmed or photographed, is not lost on me. If I had not chosen to participate in this filmed experience I am not sure how happy I would be to suddenly see a camera in my vicinity.

Patras, despite being the European Capital of Culture in 2006 and with a population hovering around 222,460, seemed a sleepy port town, with little evidence of its inhabitants on the streets, at least those within walking distance of the coach stop. We would have had to spend money travelling into the town to find a place with potential for making money to further our journey and there was no guarantee we would be successful, so we decide to keep what little cash we have for taking a boat. After much discussion, 'set-up' shots of Johan and I pouring over a map and the more relevant, not so gentle, off-camera persuasion of the producer, we decide to head to Corfu, north of Patras and en route to Italy. It wasn't our idea but it did make sense. But I also had a sneaking suspicion the producer had an alternative reason for wanting us to go there. We had successfully avoided the tourist filled bar and club areas in Athens, but would we be able to in Corfu? I'm sure it would make 'great television' to see us humiliated on a late-night bar strip, trying to busk competing with the muffled techno sounds from a myriad of packed nightclubs and holiday revellers zigzagging the streets singing lyrics from the latest Shakira summer hit. We were going to Corfu but we'd need to be careful.

Monday 2nd August DAY 3:
– PATRAS TO CORFU

It's 1.22am and I am lying on a sofa in the communal bar on a passenger ferry heading towards the island of Corfu. I'm wrapped in my sleeping bag up to my ears with my feet butted up against those of a man I have never met before who, despite the fact there are no less than ten empty sofas on which to lie down on, has chosen the other half of mine on which to (I am desperately hoping) sleep.

Oddly, considering the actual amount of time we had spent getting to know the city and its potential merits for aiding our continued survival, it had felt completely right to leave Athens. I can only assume then that the slight feeling of doubt hanging over me must have more to do with the nature of my journey; the constant pressure of being recorded and filmed. It is difficult to explain quite how it feels to know you are being watched and listened to almost constantly, particularly while so outside of your normal comfort zone in a challenging environment. We have just officially finished our second day of filming, but already it feels much longer. The amusement of being fitted each day with a small radio mike which I must wear almost constantly (we're only allowed to take them off when we sleep) has been replaced by mild irritation, and the sense of freedom we felt yesterday in at least choosing our own destiny through team decision-making has also begun to be eroded as I start to acknowledge the producer's subtle manipulation of situations.

I had, of course, expected travelling with a television crew to affect and somewhat inform aspects of this challenge. I just hadn't expected to feel so restricted, particularly so early on, by the opposing agenda of 'programme making' versus artistic challenge. While we are receiving no help whatsoever (a fact I am pleased about, otherwise this would not be a genuine challenge), I am not prepared for the unnatural demands of 'direction', which in fact make the journey even harder. For example, requests to walk down the same road twice, carrying all the equipment, in order to get shots from more than one angle. Then there are the 'listening shots' – basically pretending that I am listening when the actual conversation has finished so that they can edit this into the final version of the conversation shown on television. Basically acting.

Performing in front of an audience is something I am no stranger to as a musician, but apart from school plays (I carried off a mean Snow White in Year 2, despite a nose bleed which sadly rendered the title Snow Red more appropriate) and an accidental role in a film once (the real actress hadn't turned up and I was the only runner who could do a Mancunian accent) I have had no acting experience, and it seemed to me that some form of acting is required for these excruciating recorded nods and wry smiles. The most uncomfortable request for me so far happened today, when I was asked to 'gaze wistfully at the open seas' as the boat left Patras harbour for the six-hour overnight trip to Corfu. Gazing wistfully is not something I am prone to doing anyway and certainly not with the lens of a £90,000 HD camera almost literally stuck up my nose.

By the time this evening was drawing to a close I wondered if Johan and I had made the right decision in saving the little money we had for finding somewhere to stay in Corfu rather than getting a cabin for tonight on the boat. While the crew snuck off one by one to the relative comfort of a bunk-bedded berth, we waited it out on the outdoor deck we had been shown to when we boarded. This curious space comprised one small bar, a small swimming pool (with no water in it) and a sporadic scattering of plastic garden furniture on which to sit. The deck, unlike the swimming pool, was covered in water and this, coupled with the occasional rock of the vessel, turned the area into a sort of plastic dodgem car funfair track with tables and chairs liable to glide into passengers at any given moment.

Exhaustion setting in, I left Johan doing a portrait for a group of fellow outdoor ticket travellers he had bonded with and hoped there might be somewhere inside to grab some sleep. Joy at finding the indoor bar, coupled with the disappointment of not having looked for it earlier, and one furtive packet of crisps (dinner) later, I discovered that the camera-man, assuming I would have fallen asleep, has come to film me tucked up snoring in my little makeshift sleeping bag bed with my new sleeping buddy snoring and twitching in an early 90s techno-rave kind of way, opposite. He looks a little embarrassed to have been caught out. I am not angry but I am disappointed. It's a cheap trick and, I feel, completely unnecessary. This isn't supposed to be Big Brother, it's Sky Arts – unless I've got it wrong, in which case only three days into the trip, I'm in big trouble.

Inspecting the alarming looking bruises running up my arms (which in reality I think must be a result of me precariously clutching my music stand and cello case as I negotiate steps and uneven paths and not the upper deck furniture), I realise this is going to be the 'art of survival' for me: learning the art of dealing with becoming a TV subject. I know it is affecting Johan too. I think in some ways it's worse for him, since he is younger and has no experience at all in front of cameras. Being in the music business for over ten years has inevitably toughened me up a little and made me a little wiser to media manipulation on some level, but for Johan it is different. He is already analysing everything he says to camera and has even asked for one piece to be edited out. I feel sorry for him, sure that it is probably the one part they will keep in, although in fact he has not said anything really stupid.

Now I am sure the camera-man has retreated to his cabin I decide to try and get some sleep, I'm here and there's little I can do apart from learn to cope with these new challenges. I celebrate my ability to deal with this situation with a pre-nap biscuit I found discarded on the table opposite earlier. Pudding!

It's 6am and we have arrived. I gave up trying to sleep a while ago which ended up being lucky for me as it meant I just witnessed the most beautiful beginnings of sunrise as we sailed into Corfu. Reds and golds framing the coal black island mountains with the sea calm as a lake beneath me, and not a camera in sight to record my watching it…lovely. I have a rare moment of feeling like a normal traveller again, sailing to a new destination with adventure awaiting. I smile.

Reunited with Johan, who had ended up making forty euros sketching his new friends last night, it's still too early to get any information on where we might go or stay on the island, so we will wait until the row of travel agencies opposite the port open in a couple of hours in the small port-side café.

Johan and I both decide we are feeling frustrated. What with my amp being insufficient and therefore requiring me to perform in a way which is out of my usual remit and Johan hawking pencil sketches instead of the large oil canvas work he normally produces, we decide it is time to stage a small artistic mutiny. We've been really careful with the little money we've earned so far and lucky that Greece and Corfu are relatively cheap places to survive in. If we continue to behave like this we could afford a little B&B somewhere quiet where we can regain a little of our artistic mojo.

Another part of the challenge I hadn't really considered is the amount of trust Johan and I have to place in each other if we are to work effectively as a team, particularly with regards to money. Stef, the assistant producer, logs all earnings we make, as they will be compared to those of our opposing team in order to define a winning team at the end of the journey, but right from day one Johan has asked me to look after everything we have earnt as he's worried that he might lose it. It's a request I'm happy to oblige, heart-warmed to see him place that responsibility and trust in me. Apart from the restaurant gig on the first night, Johan has consistently been earning more with his portrait sketches, but he is happy to share the earnings equally so as to make this journey work for both of us.

Another gold star for Johan. It's odd, because though technically this is real money, earned from one or other's artistic skill, due to the nature of our journey it does not feel real – it is part of the game, a tool to help us get to the next part of the adventure. I'm relieved Johan feels the same way as me but am also conscious that at this point he is definitely the main bread-winner. I feel rude even spending money on a packet of crisps without asking him, but likewise know he does too and this mutual respect is one of the great things emerging from this adventure already.

It's too early on in the journey to say I know Johan, but I am increasingly warming to him. I don't have any brothers or sisters but it is starting to feel like I imagine having a little brother would. I feel protective towards him.

The travel agency finally opens and we have the great fortune of being offered help from a lovely girl who knows the perfect place for two tired artists. I know this is not what the producer wants but the mutiny has begun and for the first time since the challenge began we are adamant. Triumphant at having found a potentially quiet corner of the island we shoot a piece to camera showing where we intend to go. I realise I am holding the map upside down. Oh dear.

Her suggestion is spot on. We declined the producer's suggestion that we take a 'nice taxi' across Corfu, which would have meant us spending precious money we could use for an extra night's accommodation, and take a bus, which drops us at the bottom of a very steep hill. Tired, we slowly haul up all our belongings, our hard work justified when we finally make it to the top. Pelekas is perfect. The producer is not happy…

The second largest of the Ionian islands, covering 471 square miles, Corfu has a population of approximately 107,879, which swells to over a million with tourists over the summer months. Many head to resorts such as Kavos on the southern tip where they can find a selection of fantastic Irish bars and British cafés. (I've heard the baked beans are pretty good there too.) I'm sure it would make fantastic television to have Johan and me struggling our way through the drunken crowds trying to earn some money from travellers who I already know would have no interest whatsoever in what we were doing. Let's face it, if you are wooed by one euro shots of nondescript alcohol and foam parties you're probably not too bothered about a girl playing cello on the street, particularly if she is currently having to play classical music she has not practised. I've no wish to be filmed in that situation no matter how amusing the producer might find it. This journey is supposed to be about surviving using our artistic skills, not seeing how far we will go to humiliate ourselves in the name of entertaining television.

We have around 100€ left thanks to our decision not to take cabins on the boat and Johan's midnight portrait commission from the guys he met. We've discovered a little B&B we calculate we can afford for two nights if we share a twin room. It's the first time we will share accommodation but it's a compromise we're both willing to make, relieved not to be sleeping on the streets (yet!). The B&B, *Bridgette's*, is gorgeous. Located down a winding stepped path (cue tussle with cello and fresh bruises), it is a little fairytale of a Greek building, vines wrapping around walls, wind chimes and little plants randomly dotted throughout the front garden.

The room is perfect with a little outdoor balcony offering stunning views of the sea and mountains surrounding us, which Johan proclaims is ideal for preparing his canvases. It is also sufficient for us to sit and chat on while sharing a bottle of chilled wine and some bread and cheese we get from a local store to celebrate our freedom, once it becomes clear to the producer we are not giving in to manipulation and intend to stay here.

The crew retreat into the village for a few hours to find their own accommodation. Accompanied only by the intermittent sounds of the local dogs, birds and the odd lone passing scooter, Johan and I talk a bit about ourselves free from the constraints of our of radio mikes. (Although by this stage we're not convinced they haven't James Bond-style bugged the room in a futile attempt to at least get some interesting audio for the show.)

The mikes are an interesting addition to the equation. I'm used to recording and using them as a musician, but these are hidden (so as not to be viewed on camera) under our shirts. So far I have never forgotten it is there and that I am being recorded and, despite the sound-man's promise that they do not have the ability to work a certain distance from him,

I religiously unplug mine before going to the loo, just in case. I also think it makes me more cautious in how and what I say and I wonder if this will be sustainable throughout the journey or whether I will eventually completely forget it is there. Interestingly, the caution does not mean I feel the need to be someone I am not and not to say how I feel. I think Johan may be finding being recorded a bit tougher. He mentions it occasionally, and I wonder what sort of toll this may take on him and how it might affect our experience.

Johan is setting up a chaotic little art studio on the balcony, which I love. It reminds me of the years I spent at art college, which I attended during a sabbatical from the music business a few years ago in between making albums. He is stretching a large canvas that is the size of the frame he has with him but he wishes he had some smaller ones too and is cursing his choice of packing. We talk about our experience so far but also about other things. Johan brings up the subject of religion: am I religious? No, is my answer. I do not believe in God but neither do I absolutely refute the possibility that there is one. I've just had no life experience or proof there is and on this basis I chose to keep an open mind in lieu of absolute faith in the unknowable.

Johan is a born again Christian. I am curious about his views and beliefs, which I find refreshing compared to previous conversations I have had with people. He does not acknowledge guilt and sin as being part of religion, although he does have a healthy sense of needing to be responsible for your actions. He sees his faith as a purely positive thing and believes in a God

me a more sufficient amp so that I could try and busk locally and Johan would go to paint outside with the new smaller canvases he had acquired from our B&B hostess Bridgitte while I was asleep this afternoon. It was interesting that almost immediately proceeding our balcony discussion about hope and faith, this lady had provided Johan with exactly what he needed. She had had three small frames lying in her garage, but with no-one in her family painting she hadn't a clue why they were there and Johan was most welcome to them.

I managed to find an Irish bar that would not only lend me an amp but, subject to a little audition, might actually let me perform a concert to help raise money. I shall never discount the merit of such an establishment in foreign climes again – Guinness and baked beans all round...

Just as I was concluding the arrangements for my 'audition', Johan and the crew appeared. Johan had completed three small abstracts inspired by the surroundings and had subsequently sold one to a local hotel owner and collector of art. He had made 800€. This changed everything.

The first thing Johan suggests is that we use some of the money to buy me a better amp before we leave the island. I almost start to cry, he knows how important this is to me and his generosity overwhelms me. He has also met a local artist, originally from Australia, who has invited us for lunch tomorrow.

We eat with the crew in a nice restaurant near our B&B this evening. We push the boat out and feast on fresh vine leaves, meats and cheeses. Everyone is in a good mood – we made great television after all, a struggle, an adventure, a resolution. Even the producer is smiling.

After dinner we return to the Irish bar and I pass my audition. The amp, while old, aided by some expert kicks from its owner, works like a dream and for the first time I enjoy playing and feel excited by the prospect of doing the same again tomorrow with an audience.

Tuesday 3rd August DAY 4
– PELEKAS, CORFU

Another day, another feast.

There is slight embarrassment at the beginning of the lunch with our Australian hosts. 'Where's the film crew, aren't they coming for lunch too?' I am stung by an emotion I do not want to acknowledge. It is the first time we have been invited into someone's private home and I am saddened to think it may only be because of the camera and the hosts own desire for a spot of self-promotion. Whether my suspicion of their initial motive is true or not, they prove to be quite lovely and fantastic hosts. After lunch, they take us on a tour of their original Greek village house, including our host's studio and some extraordinary work which I am instantly relieved to find I genuinely like very much (I've never been good at fake pleasantries).

We sit outside and discuss the Greek philosophy on life as far as they had grown to understand it after over ten years living part-time in Pelekas (they spend the

Greek winter months back in Australia). Fuelled by the *retsina* on continuous pour and the delicious dried fruits and salads the artist's partner keeps presenting us with, we all ended up agreeing the Greeks had got something very right. Everyone seems to smile at themselves and at those around them, even though financially they're not in general, well off.

I think about my last week in London before leaving, less than a week ago but it feels like months already. It's curious how time can warp depending on the depth and intensity of human experience. I had been surrounded by people who, for the most part, had the freedom to travel, to purchase almost anything they might possibly need to survive and indulge in materialistic desires, and yet who, for all the world, seem to go about with such unhappiness. I wondered, though, whether our philosophies were really that different or whether it is just that the state of being within a society such as the one I am accustomed to is contagious and addictive. Because no-one is smiling, no-one attempts to. I'm sure if you asked most people living in London they would agree that they wished the other people they met were warmer, friendlier and enjoyed life more, and yet those same people are unlikely to crack the first smile and I have to admit that would normally mean me included.

We leave our new artist friends to join the crew for filming on the beach, taking the hand-made flyers we had prepared before our lunch date to promote my concert this evening. It's another boiling hot day and they have insisted I carry my cello with me (for visual purposes). It's not easy on the sand, which also proves impossibly hot to walk on barefoot. Eventually the producer takes pity on us and allows a brief escape into the sea. It takes me a few minutes to decide that the lure of the water is stronger than my embarrassment of being filmed in a bikini. Sadly I don't quite manage the grace or glamour of Brigitte Bardot, but the water is delicious.

It's also interesting as this is one of the first times I have been consciously concerned about my appearance on camera. I had decided from the get-go that indulging in vanity would be a disadvantage given the nature of the challenge. I also inherited a few allergies from my generous parental donors, including one that means my skin does not react well to make-up being slapped all over it. Occasionally I brave it, only to be rewarded with swollen watering eyes and, while I have had to endure its temporary application for television appearances as a musician, I avoid it personally as much as possible. So not being accustomed to the daily routine of creamy coverage, coupled with not having the luxury of packing any nice clothes, it seemed fairly pointless to get preoccupied with looking good for camera. I also didn't think it was relevant to the journey. Who cares? If the programme had been 'the art of looking good while trying to survive through Europe" maybe – but then I wouldn't have agreed to be on it (even with such a snappy title).

My concert this evening is definitely no sensory delight. Visually, in the small but perfectly formed town square, I am gifted with the perfect setting, but acoustically I am not so generously endowed. The amp owner does not appear and my kicks are clearly not so expert, neither is the decision taken by the bar owner for me to play outside apposed to my earlier audition in the interior of the bar. I struggle through a few songs for the small crowd that has gathered but it's tough, the amp crackles in and out of functioning, distorting the loop unit's recordings. But I'm warmed by the support I receive not only from Johan but also the entire crew. I can feel that they want me to succeed and it is almost worth this new defeat to feel that and hope we might be forming a closer bond as an extended team.

We all sit together and share beers post the prematurely abandoned 'concert' and I recount an experience earlier in the day when two Greek men in a Porsche (what financial crisis?) stalked me as I walked back to the B&B alone, with offers of a massage being shouted through the window. I'm still not quite sure what they were expecting. Maybe for me to be so overwhelmed by their kind and physically generous offer that I would throw my cello into the nearest ditch (there was no way it would fit in that convertible) and leap in next to them with yelps of joy at the possibility of a liaison with two, fat, middle-aged, hairy letches? Hmmm, maybe not.

The crew also share some funny stories from previous shoots. With the exception of Stef, the others have worked together before. They made a similar show to ours in America called 'Art Race'. That time there were only two competitors battling it out to survive as painters and travelling from the west to east coast of America. They told us how the pressure of filming had become too much for the artistic contributor they were assigned to film. He had staged his own artistic mutiny, choosing a strip club somewhere in Middle America for the venue, accompanied by a bottle of whiskey. Unfortunately he had forgotten about his radio mike and his parting words before the battery ran out were apparently, 'I didn't know you could get a tattoo *there...*'

I realised how nice it was to socialise again with people similar in age to me. As much as I liked Johan, there were some moments and humour that were easier to share with people nearer my own age.

Wednesday 4th August DAY 5 – PELEKAS, CORFU

I woke up this morning with a familiar nagging anxiety. Much as it had been nice to feel the crew's sympathy, I was worried. Will I be the one the viewers watch and think, 'What is she doing there? She's clearly not talented enough!' I imagined our competitors elegantly playing and singing renditions of complicated classical pieces – the cellist a veritable Jacqueline Du Pré effortlessly gliding around Europe wowing all who hear her – and thought about Johan's success and struggled to make my own experience feel positive. However, I was also aware that an amount of this was just bruised ego and also that this deeper insecurity was something I had courted irrespective of this challenge, this specific situation, for most of my creative life, realising it has also served in the past to provide a driving force for me to better myself, which has aided my creative process. Nevertheless, for the purposes of surviving this challenge, I know that I have to find a way to let it go or at least not allow it to consume me. With that in mind, Johan and I left our little B&B haven to do what a girl does best in times of stress. Shop – or in my case, as someone who's never been that keen on it as a pastime, play with things that make cool sounds in the music shop.

Johan went, accompanied by the crew, to follow a lead on a possible gallery that might be interested in the other two abstracts he had painted the other day, while I found a music shop selling amps. It became clear that I would have to buy one that required power from an electrical socket, but no-one seemed concerned by this – I think the producer was just relieved I might finally be able to make some noise. Amp purchased, Johan's lead turned out to be fruitless, but we had more than enough money left to continue our journey and celebrated this with the purchase of a tartan shopping trolley to facilitate the transportation of the new amp and Johan's newly purchased oil paint selection. The 'granny trolley' as we have fondly christened it, looks mildly ridiculous, like a giant shortbread biscuit box. It suits Johan and me perfectly. We're sure it won't last a week, let alone the next month, but it's a relatively cheap solution which works for now.

Thursday 5th August DAY 6
– CORFU – BARI, ITALY – NAPLES, ITALY

Before I left London I had wondered not just where we would travel but also what type of people we might encounter. Would anyone house us? Feed us? Would we even make any money? Could we make it all the way back to Edinburgh? I had no idea. Now, only six days in, I feel that Edinburgh is an achievable aim. Now I know my travelling companion and see our ability to communicate and work as a team, I feel a sense of optimism. I have no doubt that as long as we stay determined we will get there.

Of course, I cannot discount the influence our current financial success has on my optimistic state of mind. We are currently travelling with around 600€ in our pockets (or, more precisely, in a little green purse bag I have continually slung across me – bum bags went out in the eighties, at least I hope they did). The producer voices concerns that we now have too much money to experience the challenge authentically. Maybe he has a point: perhaps adversity would lead us to have more engaging and diverse encounters with people than we might normally. I have no idea.

One thing the crew, Johan and I are sure about is that it's time to move on from Corfu. We've decided to head to Bari, Italy, from where we can journey up through Italy and plan how to traverse northern Europe. A boat sails this evening.

It's now 1am and I'm lying in a cabin I'm sharing with Stef. This boat is easily the weirdest mode of transport I have yet encountered. From the outside, it looks like a giant tug boat with a large open car deck; everything else is housed in the hull. Unlike normal modern passenger ferries, there is nothing except a small bar, a café-style restaurant emitting some curious rotten cabbage-type odour and lots of cabins, crammed down very narrow beige metal corridors. It looks like the last refurbishment occurred sometime in the mid-fifties. The cabin is tiny with a broken plastic toilet and a sink that dribbles water with no particular relevance to whether the tap is turned on or off. There is also a small shower which functions in a similar way, producing a constant stream of water throughout the voyage. I love it.

Room inspection complete, I returned to the bar earlier this evening to have a beer with the crew, who I feel I am now starting to become friends with. We swapped stories about the worst jobs we've done. I realise that while I haven't really hated any of my jobs, I have had an extraordinarily broad range of experiences. In my early musical career I often had to take part-time jobs in between touring to earn enough to pay the rent; working as a secretary for a psychologist in a mental hospital, a librarian in a forensic science laboratory, a dish washer, a painter and decorator...seems I'd got around a bit in between the gigs and studio sessions.

Not wanting to get too drunk and risk a hangover tomorrow, I ventured out onto the large car deck. There were people with camper vans and cars sitting on fold-up chairs, playing music under the stars. Some dancing, some drinking, it was a lovely atmosphere and reminded me a bit of a UK music festival in the camping area, minus the inevitable rain, mud and pervading smell of at least thirty thousand people's urine.

We arrive at the port in Bari, the second largest city in southern Italy, at 10am. As soon as we step onto dry land we are asked to film and re-film walking through the port at least three times with all our gear. We have already decided we will not stay in Bari, choosing instead to head for Naples, a city that might prove more attractive to tourists and thus give us a potentially wider busking audience and so, already tired, we have to begin our 'real' journey, walking a good three kilometres to the train station. It's thirty-six degrees and we haven't had anything to eat or drink since the night before. I feel sick by the time we reach the main train station at 12 noon. Relieved to find a little station café, I can't remember a bottle of water ever tasting so good.

Feeling reinvigorated, I wanted to try out the new amp in the café, since there was a plug point and the owner seemed happy to let me play. However, this was not deemed 'exciting' enough for television and, 'Besides', said the producer, 'you have too much money anyway.'

However, making Johan try to get a portrait commission on the Bari to Naples train was deemed exciting enough. I was worried this would be impossible and he would feel a little humiliated, but he is turning out to be excellent at self-promotion and sales, and almost immediately finds a willing subject. I wonder if my sense of amazement every time someone agrees to pay for our artistic skills will decrease during the trip. And I wonder why I am amazed – after all, I am a professional musician. I wonder what this says about my own deeper sense of self-confidence and it makes me feel a little uneasy. I decide I am more amazed just by people's willingness to engage with complete strangers. I also allow myself to acknowledge – feeling a little ashamed – that if it were me on the train being approached I would probably not have spoken to either of us, particularly with the cameras around.

During the train ride we continue to talk about our financial state of affairs and the producer asks if we will spend all the money we have in Naples, leaving just enough to get to the nearby island of Capri. We have a rare moment of unison and agree that this might actually be an interesting plan. I was ready now to step the adventure up a gear, and quite frankly tired of constantly opposing the producer. I was feeling more confident in our ability to survive and also curious to see what might happen on an island as famously affluent as Capri if you had nothing.

Unknown to the crew or Johan, there was another reason for my capitulation. I have been to Capri before. Last Easter, the Ex and I had been there for a short break. It had been an interesting experience. Beautiful as the landscape had been, I had found the atmosphere strange, too many designer labels and people wanting to 'be seen', and not enough laughter or visible signs of enjoyment, not my kind of town. I was extremely curious to revisit this place under completely different circumstances.

LATER

Apparently, tonight is 'all about me'. We checked in, with the crew, at the most expensive hotel we could find in Naples once we had arrived, which means that except for our boat fare to Capri tomorrow, we are pretty much penniless again. Armed with my new amp, on the recommendation of the hotel concierge we head for the most famous bar in town, 'Café Gambrinus'. One time haunt of such illustrious figures as Oscar Wilde and Gabriele D'Annunzio, the café celebrated its 150th birthday earlier in the year by reviving an old Neapolitan tradition, the *café sospeso*. This custom means a customer paying his or her bill also paying for an extra coffee. These extra coffees would then be consumed by the poor or homeless who would come in and ask for a *café pagato* (a 'paid-for coffee') or *café sospeso* (a 'coffee in suspense', i.e, waiting for someone to need it).

This kind of sentiment is exactly why I love Italy. I have always loved the place, since the first time I visited with a friend of mine whose family had a house in Tuscany, which I visited one summer in my early twenties. There are many things I find beautiful about the Italian way of life and pretty high up on my list definitely has to be '*aperitivo* time'.

'*Aperitivo* time' mustn't be confused with the British 'happy hour', where drinks (normally the cheapest ones) are further discounted, a clever ruse to get you very drunk very quickly so you then stay and consume full-price premium drinks for the rest of the evening. No,

Italian *aperitivo* is a much more civilised affair, where you might pay a little more for your drink but then have access to a range of bar snacks. These also mustn't be confused with my home country's offering of 'piss nuts' (come on, you know that old man in the corner on his fifth pint of ale, shoveling the free peanuts left in a bowl on the bar, didn't just wash his hands on returning from the toilet). In Italy, the snacks are a tantalising array of canapés: delicious little vol-au-vents, mini omelettes and meats and cheeses, designed to be an appetizer to tempt the palette preceding dinner. In reality, it's a veritable banquet in itself.

So we decide a good strategy is to play at the café during *aperitivo* time, when there should be plenty of people to listen. But our timing is off, *aperitivo* is over and while the amp works fairly well there are few people watching. Yet again I am filmed failing and this time, despite my best efforts to try and hide it, my disappointment is visible when I am interviewed to camera after packing down my equipment.

Then a strange and beautiful thing happened. Three Bangladeshi men with a little stall opposite the bar selling cheap trinkets had been watching. They approached me and handed me a small pink plastic digital watch. At first I thought they were trying to sell it to me, but then they explained it was a gift for the 'beautiful music'. It was worth ten euros and almost the tackiest thing I'd ever seen, but to me right then it was the best present I'd ever had. Their kindness took me out of my self-pitying revelry and renewed my confidence. I would turn this around – there was a reason I was picked for this show and I would prove it. Thanking them profusely and after much hugging and smiles, I decided to walk and see what other opportunities might present themselves in early evening Naples. With Johan (who had also been a massive support throughout the preceding struggle) and crew in tow, I took to the surrounding streets.

Naples is a mad place. There are around one million people in the main part of the city and, I would estimate, at least three rubbish sacks per person, which are conveniently left scattered all over the Neapolitan streets. This means that walking around Naples is a bit like taking part in a horizontal slalom, avoiding the near-to-bursting sacks which threaten to engulf you with their contents if you take just one misplaced step. But it's an exciting place to visit – maybe its inhabitants get their energy from being geographically sandwiched between two volcanic areas.

After successfully negotiating one particularly densely black-sack-packed narrow street, I saw a small and crowded bar filled with laughing Italians. They were having a closing down party and when I asked if I could play they accepted immediately. Indoors the amp worked beautifully, and the crowd loved the music, my own compositions looped. For the first time since I started this journey I had a cheering crowd and a smiling crew and Johan. I felt a sudden rush of joy I realised I had not experienced in months.

This time just over two weeks ago I had been begging the Ex to try and make things work. Since then, I had applied for and been accepted on this challenge, and now found myself triumphantly being filmed performing a concert in a Neapolitan bar about to embark on the most intense part of our voyage into the unknown: being broke in Capri. I couldn't wait.

Friday 6ᵗʰ August DAY 7
– NAPLES – CAPRI

It is now exactly a week since I left London for Athens, willing myself to have the courage to get on the plane and embark on this adventure. I draw open the heavy curtains of the five star hotel picked by our producer and crew and am rewarded with a spectacular view of the bay of Naples. I can't believe I am here. I realise I have completed the biggest part of the challenge already, allowing myself to take part, and I know too that only I can make it into an enjoyable adventure. Despite the worries and problems of working with television, if I allow myself, I can make this challenge into the experience of a lifetime, something to never forget.

Johan and I make our way to the port late in the morning, delayed by waiting for the crew to shoot 'GVs' (general views) of Naples, which they will intercut with the footage of us for the final TV show. It is another beautiful hot sunny day and I steal some time to myself on the short boat crossing to Capri. Just before leaving the UK, I somehow managed to work out not only how to switch on the iPhone but also how to download some albums. I decide to let the Sneaker Pimps' *Becoming X* accompany me on my aquatic portion of the journey; an interesting choice, because it had been the soundtrack to my first big tour with a band back in 1998. I remember sitting at the back of the upstairs part of the very rock and roll tour bus (complete with, I kid you not, full sized fridge and beds) looking out of the tinted back window, watching the M4 motorway being swallowed up by the miles, feeling an exciting mix of ambition and anticipation. We were on our way to perform at Glastonbury and I couldn't believe I was getting to play there. I realise being here now, feeling the spray of the sea hitting me in the face, that I have a similar feeling of youthful excitement and expectation I had not often encountered in the twelve years since that gig.

It's now 3.29am and I am in a splendid hotel room in Ana Capri, the smaller of Capri's two main towns. Less than four hours ago I had been preparing to sleep rough on one of the most affluent islands in the world.

It had been a tough start. The boat journey had been beautiful until I was rudely awakened from my revelry by my phone ringing – it was the Ex.

At first I couldn't believe it. What could be the odds of him calling just as I was arriving in Capri, our holiday destination of a year before? Here I was trying to exorcise a few ghosts from our relationship and via a mobile phone connection, he was all too suddenly here as well. He sounded fed up, particularly when I revealed my location. He was ill, had injured himself carrying too much moving his things out of our old flat. After clarifying there was absolutely nothing he needed me to do to help, I went to join Johan and the crew and felt a sense of relief at being with them.

After disembarking the boat and negotiating the narrow funicular with all our luggage, up to the main town of Capri, we started with earnest, heading straight for the heart of the town, Piazza Umberto. It took approximately eight seconds to find out that busking is strictly forbidden on the island and another ten to realise that we were therefore in very serious trouble. We now had only twenty-four euros between us and absolutely no way of making money.

I left Johan setting up a canvas to paint over-looking the sea, after we had established that as long as he didn't paint for money he was free to work outside. I, meanwhile, decided a proactive approach was required. If I couldn't busk I'd have to try and find a venue to play in that evening if I stood any chance at all of making any money.

With no venues immediately apparent (it's not always easy to spot them in the day time, since they tend to favour narrow alleyways and little signage), I ended up strolling around the white narrow streets aimlessly. Devoid of any ability to purchase, I realise what a boring, mind-numbing pursuit window shopping really is.

But then, even armed with a credit card I'm not particularly girly when it comes to shopping. Crowded department stores and frantic changing rooms have never really held any lure for me. In fact, such is my dislike of shopping that I buy almost all my clothes and shoes from the same shop. I go there twice a year when the sales are on and I don't even visit the changing room; I know the sizes and I stock up for the coming year, breathing a sigh of relief when I am on the tube home and know it's six months until I might need to venture into consumer land again. My only exceptions to this rule are music shops and food shops – I could spend hours in both. In the former, plucking strings and checking out the latest recording gear and, in the latter, indulging in the smells and sights of roasting chickens and freshly baked bread, squeezing fresh fruits and buying things in jars it turns out I'm not brave enough to eat.

I was particularly struck by how pointless and lifeless the designer window displays were, all vying for the attention of potential moneyed customers. But I must be in the minority in my opinion because as I left the town centre in search of the stunning cliff top views I remembered from my previous trip, the crowds gave way to empty streets. I climbed with the cello until I reached a secluded viewing point over-looking the bay. Here I sat down on a small stone bench and began to play.

I don't know what I was playing: not classical, not pop, just jamming sounds with no-one to listen except the ants crawling over my feet. Despite the heat, I felt comfortable and relieved to be away from the camera and crew and the sense of feeling spare due to my inability to be able to busk and help provide. At some point a woman joined me on the bench to read. She was dressed as a maid and I'm guessing, unless she was on her way to a fetish party, she was working in one of the local villas. She gave me a gummy smile which I returned (plus teeth). I thought that although we were in the cheap seats, we were far richer, and our view far better than any seen from the soundless piazza full of the see-to-be-seen drinking ten euro cappuccinos.

The walk back to the centre of town and to Johan and the crew threw up a couple of leads for possible evening venues, but I'd have to wait until they opened at 11.30pm to find out if it would be possible to play. I also spotted a small contemporary gallery I thought might be useful for Johan to visit tomorrow. At 8pm with the sun setting, we still had no earnings and an amount of money that might have been able to feed us in Greece, but definitely not here in Capri.

During my town centre reconnaissance earlier, I'd found a stand offering free copies of the local tourist magazine (a sort of *Time Out* 'Capri style') in which I'd read an article about a club here, *Anema e Core*, owned and run by a man called Guido Lembo. The article's photos showed a middle-aged, bespectacled guitarist snapped in various poses on stage with well-known international artists, and the text read:

'His charisma and irresistible charm never fail to get the throng on the dance floor going, with well-known industrialists, politicians and celebrities from the world of sport and show business often to be seen dancing at his side.'

I wondered what my chances were (rocking up with a hoodie, oil paint-stained t-shirt and cello) of getting a paid concert there tonight. I thought incredibly slim, but with few other options it had to be worth a go.

In my absence, Johan had done an amazing amount of work on his large portrait. It was of a girl he had photographed at the port in Patras, and was quite stunning. It was interesting that, like me, when the going got a bit tough he instantly defaulted to creating, finding a safety in being and working with his talent, as I had done jamming alone at the viewing point earlier. His work was attracting some attention, and one admirer turned out to be a real angel for us.

Chiara was also an artist and, we would later find out, an aspiring philosopher. We told her about our challenge and were subsequently invited for dinner. She seemed like a lovely girl and we couldn't afford to eat properly otherwise, so why not?

As daylight gave way to darkness we trekked back up through the town and up the hill to a beautiful house at the top of the island. The crew left us to get their own sustenance while we joined Chiara for a deliciously simple meal of chicken, rice and red wine. We talked about art and music and the relationship between them. Chiara said she felt it was incredibly important to let your art into the world once you had created it and not be tempted to try and hold onto it. I am deeply in agreement with this and realised that I'd been feeling frustrated about the amount of opportunity I'd been provided with to share my music over the past couple of years. Promises by my independent record label to release and distribute my last album had not lived up to expectations and a body of work I had been incredibly proud of was still almost completely unknown. It struck me that this challenge was finally providing me with at least some guaranteed platform from which to share my music, but this was coupled with the frustration of how limited I felt by the equipment I was having to use on this journey. An interesting irony, as I had previously had all the technological assistance I needed, but no audience. Right now I have a tendency, familiar to many musicians, of erring on the side of being a little too perfectionist, and I have to admit I was finding this new handicap the less preferable of the two options. But I make a decision that this is precisely why I must try to find a way to make this work – after all, I may never again have the opportunity of exposing my creativity in this way.

Chiara's parents arrived home later on and recommended a local restaurant where I could try and play. Half-an-hour later I had made seventy euros; I had decided to ditch the easy classical music for a piece I had written myself on the viewing point earlier in the day, which proved to be a success with the audience at the outdoor trattoria. Buoyed by this small triumph, I decided it was time to head for Guido's club.

Camera, crew and Chiara in tow, we walked back into town through the streets, now transformed into a buzzing evening playground for the island's wealthier inhabitants and visitors. We rounded a bend to find a long queue of some of the most bizarrely-dressed people I have ever seen. The window displays I had seen earlier in the day had now transformed themselves into moving manifestations of excruciatingly expensive bad taste. Men in leopard-skin Dolce & Gabbana t-shirts and women in ill-fitting dresses and shoes studded with Swarovski diamantes, smoking long, thin menthol cigarettes, thronged outside the place to be – the one and only *Anema e Core*.

My earlier worries were unfounded. I should have known that a man as obviously self-publicising as Guido would embrace the chance to have a film crew in his establishment. We were a welcome addition, another factor helping to maintain an atmosphere of glamour and celebrity to justify the exorbitant drink prices.

The winding stair entrance to the club gave way to a giant white-washed cave, with a large bar to the right covered in photographs of Guido with various famous actors, actresses, musicians and politicians. It appeared Guido had even managed to persuade Pavarotti to sing with him there.

I was about to perform on the huge stage to the left of the bar. Guido was already up there belting out covers of cheesy Italian pop songs, much to the delight of the inebriated entrepreneurs, models and the generally well-heeled, who were waving their Gucci scarves and clapping their Bulgari-clad hands. Our formidable host was accompanied by no less than three professional backing singers and a brass ensemble, as well as the normal band set-up.

No sooner had I had time to digest this scene than I was been hoisted onto the stage next to Guido, where it became immediately clear that I would not be performing my own music. It was decided that I would sing *I Will Survive* with Guido and the band. I didn't know the words – it didn't matter. I made them up, belting out something that vaguely resembled Gloria's track, dressed in my finest t-shirt and two euro flip flops. The crowd loved it and, to be honest, I loved it for the sheer madness of the situation, even though I was painfully aware that this ridiculous performance had just been recorded for TV. Afterwards, the producer kept muttering the words 'TV Gold' under his breath: he loved it too.

Guido turned out to be a nice man and, with his blessing, we went round the crowd with a hat and left the building a triumphant 184€ richer. We celebrated with a drink in the bar opposite, which was also filled with pictures of its owner with various celebrities. Stef and I have been inspired by tonight's show of fashion faux pas and have decided to enter into a bad taste clothing competition together – whatever hideous garments we find between now and Edinburgh, we are challenging each other to wear for the final show. Easier for her, I'll be filmed wearing them, but it's too hilarious a challenge not to take up and I'm in a good mood. In total I had made 254€ tonight. It felt good to be the one providing the income, particularly as we had so desperately needed it earlier today.

Saturday 7th August DAY 8
– CAPRI – ROME

Hotel breakfast buffets have become a tactical triumph. I have started to evaluate the strength of our accommodation not on the quality of the bed, bathroom or facilities available, but on the potential for pilfering enough food to sustain us for the day from the buffet.

There are a few factors I have decided are essential.

First, that the breakfast room is large enough, and with few enough staff, that you can hunt and gather unobserved. Second, that there are quality napkins, as you will need something to protect your food. (Paper ones are useless; by lunchtime your edible swag will have become umbilically attached to the paper, giving your stolen snacks an extra pulpy indigestible skin.) The third and most obvious factor is the quality of the sustenance on offer.

Needless to say, on this island of plenty – bordering excess – it was pretty good. Burying my shame at attaining a standard of kleptomania Oliver Twist's captor Fagin would have been proud of, I gleefully packed my usefully multi-pocketed army trousers full of fruit and cotton napkin-entombed sandwiches and joined the team for our daily strategy meeting.

Yesterday Johan managed to finish his oil portrait, which is stunning. Approximately a metre square of female face distressed with confident sweeps of colour. The plan is for Johan to go to the gallery I spotted in the centre of Capri town yesterday and see if he can sell them the piece.

It seems at first a fairly impossible challenge. Normally an artist would first have meetings with a gallery and develop a relationship, a little like a musician booking concerts. It is not done to simply walk in off the street and try to sell your work. But after our impromptu successes, with Johan selling to the collector in Corfu and me crashing Guido's club, anything seems possible right now. Either way, we have nothing to lose in trying.

Four hours and an equally dazzling boat journey

back to mainland Italy later, I'm sitting outside a small bar in Naples next to the main train station. Purely based on the sight before me I have decided to up my quota of rubbish sacks per head to five. Here the taxis and cars are also playing slalom, avoiding the sacks that have escaped into the road since they have no more pavement left on which to rest their bulging, detritus-filled contents. The air is filled with the sound of car horns, which could be considerate Neapolitan warnings from one driver to another, alerting each other to the fact there's a black plastic boulder straight ahead in the middle of the road – but I suspect it might be more to do with the southern Italian fiery impatience I find oddly charming compared to my own country's polite repressed anger in traffic jams.

Johan is sitting opposite me and we are grinning madly at each other, drinking cold *café cremas*. We have not stopped grinning since Johan sold his painting to the gallery, I discovered, for 2300€ in Capri earlier today. I have the cash inside my little green purse slung across my shoulder. With regards to potential for being robbed I am pretty sure I am currently sitting in one of the worst places in the world. We are waiting for the crew, and even though the group of men sitting on the table next to us look like something straight out of a Brian De Palma gangster film, my anxiety is quelled by the overwhelming feeling I have that luck is on our side. We have decided to head for Rome by train this evening.

Sunday 8ᵗʰ August DAY 9
– ROME

Today is officially our 'day off'. Which seems funny as of course we are still travelling. There's no possibility of going home and spending a day with my friends and, besides, I realise even if I could I wouldn't want to. The 'day off' really exists to give the crew a well-earned break, so there will be no filming today. Our microphones have been packed away and the camera is locked in one of the five star hotel rooms we are booked into, which Johan and I can now easily afford to stay in for a night or three. It wouldn't have been our choice of accommodation but, as with our first night in Naples, 'gentle persuasion' from the producer has us booked into the same hotel as them. Apart from this luxury, though, we are hoping to spend our new-found wealth on something more worthwhile in furthering our journey. Maybe today Johan and I can come up with a plan, away from the influence of the TV crew.

I spent the morning alone exploring Rome, capital of Italy, the 'eternal city'. It really is incredible. It is the only place I know where you literally feel like you are taking a walk through history, two and a half thousand years of it. Originally the capital of the Roman Kingdom, home of the Pope and the Vatican City (an independent city-state run by the Catholic Church) the centre is, deservedly, a UNESCO world heritage site.

There's the Roman-constructed Pantheon, which was completed in 120 AD and is still a working church; medieval basilicas, such as the Santa Maria

Maggiore with her fifth century AD mosaics; some of the finest examples of Renaissance and Baroque Art, sculpture and architecture in the world, including the Trevi Fountain by Nicola Salvi (opposite which there also happens to be one of the world's finest examples of ice-cream vendor); and brilliant examples of Fascist architecture, such as the Palazzo della Civiltà Italiana, also known as the cubic or square colosseum, built between 1938-1943. This is, of course, not to mention the fine array of ancient statues, obelisks and columns that seem to greet you on almost every street in the city centre. In fact it is the modernisation of the city that is proving difficult. The construction of a new metro line being built through the centre to ease congestion has been stalled numerous times due to discoveries of more ancient artifacts each time they attempt to dig the tunnel.

As I explored – no baggage, no crew, no cameras, no Johan – I had a sudden moment of exhilaration. Not just because of the splendid solitude, but also because I suddenly felt incredibly proud. I had not sat in London licking my wounds, I had taken on a challenge and so far I was surviving. I realised I had not felt this sensation of excitement and pure happiness in a very long time.

I met with Johan after lunch and we continued exploring the city together. We decided to brave the queue for the Colosseum and were duly rewarded for our patience. Built in 70-80 AD, it is the largest amphitheatre ever built in the Roman Empire. Originally it could have housed around 50,000 spectators and now welcomes over four million tourists a year. Despite the fact that the Colosseum is now a shadow of its former self, it is still a formidable sight. Especially when you are armed with the knowledge of the historic acts of cruelty that took place inside in the name of entertainment.

I had to admit there were times on this trip now where I was starting to wonder just what I had got myself into. I might not have anyone back home waiting with a bunch of peeled grapes (but then I suspect in reality neither did the Gladiators, let's call that paragraph artistic license), but did that really justify taking myself so far out of my comfort zone? How will my life change when this show eventually airs? Will people be allowed to see the true journey or will it be edited in a way purely to provide the most entertainment for the audience? And will that audience be kind in their judgment or will we be metaphorically stoned by them?

I can see that I am trading my much-prized anonymity and selling myself as entertainment in order to leave a situation I had not seen a better way out of. I had always found comfort and an escape from feeling alone in attempting to communicate with people through my music – and, of course, when you break up with someone, apart from the initial feelings of hurt and bruised ego, the one thing that can remain, the worst thing a human being can feel, after physical pain, is loneliness.

Monday 9th August DAY 10
– ROME

When I finally made it to university at the grand old age of twenty-nine, during a temporary musical career break, I developed a passion for studying the relationship between music and visual art. (Hardly surprising, with a career in the former and a degree specialising in the latter.) In the nineteenth century, Walter Pater (an English essayist and Art literary critic) said, 'The arts are able, not indeed to supply the place of each other, but reciprocally to lend each other new forces', and concluded that, 'All art should aspire to the condition of music.'

I was hugely inspired at art college by a number of people who seemed to have put Pater's words into practice. For example, the composer Wagner, who aspired in his later work to create *gesamtkunstwerk*, a kind of art which combines all other forms, and the painter Wassily Kandinsky, whose frequent correspondence with the composer Arnold Schoenberg led to the former's attempts to 'musicalise' a painting through the medium of abstract art.

Another artist, a contemporary of Kandinsky's who would later go on to teach with him at the famous Bauhaus design school, was the Swiss-born painter Paul Klee. A number of his works were created using a series of transparent overlapping layers of paint which he referred to as 'polyphony', a term used to describe music containing parts of equal significance which are played simultaneously.

For my own first attempt at working with both

colour and music, I turned to the science of Sir Isaac Newton. In 1704, through his analysis of the properties of sunlight, Newton divided the spectrum into seven colours, one for each note of the musical scale:

A – Blue
B – Indigo
C – Violet
D – Red
E – Orange
F – Yellow

He worked this out based on the relationship between refraction of light and sonic frequency. So, for example, the colour red has the lowest degree of refraction, while the note D has the lowest frequency. In this way, colour and sound were united in one mathematical matrix.

My project brief at college had been to base a visual project around the word 'collection', inspired by a visit to a museum in Oxford housing an extraordinary collection of objects acquired by the anthropologist Pitt Rivers. My inspiration, however, came from the amount of times I observed people being told off by the museum staff for letting their mobile phones ring. Shelving the inevitable guilt arising from fastidiously ignoring the numerous beautiful artifacts on display in favour of the sounds emitted by a load of twenty-first century plastic devices, I decided I would use this as the basis for my project. I would take a 'collection' of twenty ringtones from mobile phones and score out their tunes. Referring to Newton's study, I would then represent the notes visually as blocks of colour, taking into consideration the length of note, frequency of use and each note's position within the tune. Purely to add another aesthetic element to the project, I also recorded each ringtone into my computer and sketched the shape of the sound wave each one produced. For reasons still unbeknown to me, after collating all this information I decided to make a huge wall piece out of layers and layers of coloured card, which required me cutting up boxes for roughly one month. By the end I had suffered a sort of scissor-wielding induced repetitive strain injury and two disturbing looking dents on my fingers which were visible for several months afterwards. The project was deemed a success by my tutors, but I still feel a bit queasy around cutting implements or cardboard packaging.

By the time I graduated from college, I already had my next record contract signed and with the shift of focus away from visual art, I suspended further personal investigation of the representation of art through music.

But now, suddenly here I am travelling through Europe with a visual artist, with no specific obligation to produce anything other than original material. I realise I am finally provided with a scenario that might allow me to revisit this subject. I had tentatively been asking Johan if he would be interested in us collaborating during the course of the trip and, while I wasn't met with resistance, I could feel a slight apprehension on his part. It was understandable – I was asking him to go out of his artistic comfort zone, and be filmed doing so.

So I am delighted that Johan has decided to use some of our new-found wealth to fund our first collaboration.

A plan has been hatched.

There is a famous piazza in Rome called Piazza Navona. It is a beautiful example of Baroque design and the perfect setting for our collaboration. Although we were making an early start, it was already hot and crowded with tourists and street artists selling work around the square. It reminded me of the first time I went to Paris with my parents when I was twelve. We went to the *Montmatre*, which was also crowded with artists with makeshift stalls selling paintings. There were hundreds of brightly-coloured canvases, many depicting the surrounding area, and I remember watching from a little café as the tourists left their lunchtime tables and diverged on the stands like ants crawling across garden pavement slabs. I had found it so exciting to see such a buzz of activity and to be able to get so close to paintings; in London I had only seen them hanging in galleries, their shiny oil painted surfaces tantalisingly out of reach.

We found a space at one end of the square where Johan proceeded to lay out a large canvas, with the intention of painting an abstract in response to the environment. After an interview to camera explaining what we were about to do, Johan began to squeeze colours from his tubes of oil paints – and, as he did so, I noted which colours he chose in which order, the amount of colour applied and the length of time he took with each application. I also tried to observe just how he applied the paints: long strokes, short strokes, lines, dots.

We spent the whole morning working in this way, and

in our breaks I tried to find a studio that would allow me to work on recording my musical response to the work. Happily, I found a small studio on the outskirts of Rome willing to donate a few hours of time and an engineer. It turned out the studio was in the home of the engineer, a lovely man called Vinx, who ended up giving up all evening to record three tracks with me. I had chosen to split my musical response into three parts, as Johan had produced his abstract in three stages (applying a layer, allowing it to dry and observing, and repeating this processes an additional two times).

It was an intense process. I was trying to interpret as accurately as possible from my notes and produce something of the quality normally achieved in a week or so in a professional studio. I also had to bear in mind that if I wanted to replicate the work live I was limited with the small loop unit and would have to incorporate this way of working into the recording process. But somehow, by midnight, five hours later, and despite the delays caused by the film crew recording us, a CD had been made. Vinx had charged nothing for his time and was incredibly professional and kind. Returning to the centre of town, although exhausted, I had too much adrenalin to sleep and spent an hour wandering the streets of Rome, eating pizza from one of the late-night bakeries. I was amazed at what could be achieved in one day if you really tried: a CD, an abstract painting and, excluding material costs, none of it had technically cost a penny.

Janie Price

Tuesday 10th August DAY 11
– ROME – MONTEPULCIANO (TUSCANY)

It is 8.47pm and the producer, Johan and I are on another train.

We arrived at *Stazione di Roma Termini* around 7pm with a vague notion of heading to Tuscany. As we were still fairly cash rich we wanted to find some way to inject a little more adventure into the journey, and decided we would allow the ticket vendor at the station to pick the precise location for us.

He was very amused by the randomness of our request. Understandable; generally people buying tickets to travel know where they want to go. He also wins the award for the happiest ticket vendor I have ever met, chuckling and whistling his way through suggestions with bonhomie. I see that encountering people like him is starting to change the way I view the world; that there are a lot more happy, helpful people about than I had realised.

Here in possibly the oldest train carriage in the world (I can't believe anything pre-this-design exists that wasn't powered by animals), forty-eight copies of my CD sit proudly in my rucksack, titled, after lengthy discussion earlier today, *Painting with Music (A Responsive Collaboration between Artist and Composer)*. Not the most inspired title, I'll admit, but with limited time and other suggestions including the producer's enthusiastic wordplays on my instrument of choice – *One Chell of a Journey, Highway to Chell, Cello, Goodbye* – I think we got off quite lightly with the final choice.

We invested a little money in blank CD cases and printing, choosing a digital photo of Johan's abstract I had taken on my phone to illustrate the CD and case. The printing shop we found, somewhere a little outside the centre of Rome, was run by another man in line for a happiness award. Not only did he give us the printed covers at a discount (in exchange for a copy of the CD), he also let us use his computer to format the covers and turn his little shop into a virtual CD production factory, as we cut and inserted the artwork into the cases we had bought earlier. It was lunchtime when we finished and he then took us to a local restaurant where he ate lunch every day.

Another thing the Italians definitely have right is *il pranzo* (lunchtime). While back in the UK, millions of us rush from our places of work sometime between twelve and two to the nearest high street sandwich retailer, inevitably wasting half of our precious allotted break trying to get to the relevant shelf in the shop, along with what seems like one hundred or so other desperately hungry workers, and almost the entire other half queuing, leaving approximately five minutes back at the desk to consume said purchase (which wasn't what you had been looking forward to all morning anyway as the man behind you had snatched it from before your eyes with his freakishly long arms), the Italians are having a fantastic time dining in a lovely local restaurant.

Us northern Europeans have been investigating the 'Mediterranean Diet' and its links to happiness and longevity for some time now. But I think we've been missing one key point; it's not just the type of food you consume, but how you consume it. The best way is slowly, with laughter and friends around, maybe even a little glass of red on the side. You too would be happy in your work and willing to work a little later in the evening if you had a two-hour feast each day with your best mates.

After a simple, gorgeous lunch, Stef and I stumble across a fantastic one euro clothing stall packed with items suitable for our bad taste competition. Wild-eyed and excited, we grabbed at animal print clothing like women possessed. And one pair of snake skin leggings, some leopard print lycra pants and – the piece de la resistance – a mixed animal print shirt later, we were ready to return to the centre of Rome for an interview on my and Johan's progress, more 'acting shots' – and walking up and down streets numerous times.

Then another random moment. The problem with these moments is that they feel as unbelievable for us as I am sure, if any of them make the final cut for the show, they will for the audience. The thing is, and I'm afraid you really are just going to have to believe me on this one, they are completely genuine.

We were in the narrow street next to the hotel we had been staying at for the past two nights. Johan's large abstract from the piazza yesterday was laid out on the pavement and we were sitting on a doorstep being filmed sharing our first joint listening of the finished CD. To be fair, I shouldn't have been surprised that our little street set-up attracted some attention, but the chances of one of the group of observers being an art collector? That had to be slim. Smartly, stylishly dressed in the casual and seemingly effortless way all Italians seem to be born with the ability to carry off, he was interested in Johan's work but put off by the scale of it (at over two-and-a-half metres wide this was fair enough). But he left his card with Johan anyway and walked away. Two minutes later Johan had an idea: what about the smaller Corfu abstracts? He still had two left. He called the collector who, it turned out, was still not far away and agreed to return to see the smaller pieces. A handshake and exchange of 500€ later, we were down to one Corfu abstract and a shell-shocked producer and me.

We've just arrived in the Tuscan town of Montepulciano, and the only signs of life are displaying themselves in the train station café/bar which, I conclude after being refused entrance, is the most unlikely private members' club in the world. There is no taxi rank, but there is an old, torn poster on the wall with taxi numbers. It's our only lead, so I call one of them. I manage to negotiate something with my pidgin Italian. I think he will be arriving in ten minutes. But there is also the chance the conversation translated went something like this:

'Good evening.' (Me)
'Good evening!!!'(Super-enthusiastic cabbie)
'I need to post a letter, you a car?'
'Ah, crazy English tourist, you need a cab. I bet you are at the deserted train station with the private bar you cannot enter!'
'I am at the train station, how much are you?'
'Ah, glad you asked, because I charge triple for tourists

and will undoubtedly keep you waiting at least half-an-hour while I go for a pre-drive *aperitivo* at my friend's house.'

'Thank you!'

'No, thank you... !'

Half-an-hour later, a shiny new red jaguar pulls up. Our taxi driver is apparently the film star Robin Williams, or at least looks just like him. After successfully completing the Mensa-style test of fitting all our belongings into the smallest car boot in the world, we head to the centre, parched and willing there to be at least one drinking establishment in town we don't need a membership card to get into.

The centre of Montepulciano was thankfully considerably livelier than our point of arrival. We checked into the world's most confusing hotel, which was built downwards into a hill. The lift button numbers were consequently all wrong and had been covered with sticky labels in an attempt to rectify the matter, which in fact only confused things more. Making a mental note to use the stairs for the rest of my stay, I rejoined Johan and the crew in the lobby and we decided to venture over to the square opposite, lured by the sounds of live music and the smell of pizza. In the square, we chanced upon the end of a festival, where a large tent had been set up, housing a bar and games room. Johan revealed his competitive side with a nail-biting table tennis tournament – but, unfortunately, the ten-year-old Italian lad proved too tough a challenger for my bare-footed artist friend. Stef and I had more success in a pool tournament against two friendly, toothless Romanians. (I still have no idea how they ate the pizza they ordered at the end of the match; maybe they just sucked off the topping...)

Wednesday 11th August DAY 12
– MONTEPULCIANO (TUSCANY) – MONTICCHIELLO (TUSCANY)

This morning's breakfast buffet proved a bitter blow for the self-confessed buffet kleptomaniac. I tried to cheer myself up by placing a dried prune on top of the stale cereal I had decided was the only vaguely edible option on offer.

The camera-man (who has become my breakfast buddy on account of him being the only other early riser in our team) is not having much luck either. My caffeine-addicted companion, upon asking for his habitual four shots of espresso in one cup, has been denied his usual morning kick. Apparently there is a quota per head. I offer my 'quota' (I'm guessing it's two cups each?), but this is not permitted either. We decide to wait for the rest of the crew, who promptly order double espressos and give them to the camera-man, thankfully just before the symptoms of cold turkey begin to display themselves. Judging from the average age of our fellow diners, there is already quite enough dribbling and shaking going on in this room on a daily basis.

The producer has decided to call Robin Williams,

now undercover as an Italian cab driver. To continue our theme of random destinations, we will allow him to suggest a village we should head to for the day.

Robin Williams turns out to be a) slightly mad and b) very patient. The crew spent ages trying to place a little mobile camera (called a 'GoPro') on his shiny car to film the journey. It was decided Johan and I would travel alone with the cab driver, followed in cat-and-mouse pursuit by the crew and main camera in the Range Rover. During the journey, poor Mr Williams was constantly asked to stop on bends and to wait for the crew car, via a series of mobile phone calls from the producer, so they could get the right shots.

During this fragmented journey he chatted away to us in broken English (which was still much better than my Italian). He told us he is not allowed to go to southern Italy as he did 'something naughty during national service'. He also repeatedly asked me if I had a boyfriend while 'accidently' brushing against my leg with his hand. The GoPro mobile camera wasn't angled to record this, but instead was shooting my face, so I spent the entire journey grinning wildly, pretending to enjoy the scenery while batting away my naughty friend's advances. Needless to say, the trip felt very long.

We eventually arrived in the small-but-perfectly-formed town of Montecchiello, our driver's destination of choice.

It's now early evening and I'm currently hiding in a small bar/restaurant perched on top of a hill at the entrance to the town. I am wedged on a stool between my cello and an ice cream fridge, which is clearly irritating one of the two bar staff, but it is the only space in the place. I'm eating bar nuts (no ale-drinking old men in sight so I think they are safe) and drinking a cold beer. I need it. I'm hot and tired after walking to and from our B&B with all my gear, which ended up being a lot further away than was described earlier.

I also needed a break from the rest of the team and, in particular, the producer. He is surprised by how well we are doing and is again concerned this means we are not making exciting enough television. On our way from Rome, he had suggested that we should try to spend some of our money at the next destination. In order to do this, we decided we would like to do something that somehow gave something to a community. But strolling into a town and simply donating money didn't seem like the right thing to do. To start with, we wouldn't have time to find out where the money might be needed most, if at all. So we decided we would aim to put on a show. We would spend a day or two recording the local life through visual and audio studies and then invite the community to a party we would host. We could have a performance and exhibition, hire a local hall or space and buy locally-produced food and drinks for the evening.

The problem was, our random destination was already buzzing with events. Our visit happened to coincide with a week of outdoor theatre performances in the small village centre. Furthermore, the producer was dissatisfied with the 'look' of the village; it was 'too pretty' (a nonsensical criticism in my view). I tried to explain, bearing in mind my previous trips to Tuscany, that pretty villages seemed to be the norm in this region. If he wanted 'ghetto' it might be wiser to wait until we were somewhere else.

Again his mantra of 'you've got too much money' was repeated and suddenly I felt worn out. I am perplexed. I thought the point of the show was to explore what art is worth and if we can survive from our art alone. Therefore making money is surely one of only two ways the challenge can go. I realise I am working within complete contradiction, because us having money does not provide the producer with the drama it is all too apparent he wants for the show. I can tell this contradiction is affecting Johan too. It is like being at school and being told your grades are too high.

I can feel manipulation in my interviews to camera too. Today I was asked if I thought we were being risky enough, and was told the producer had heard the other team were being much riskier. I gave a measured but audibly irritated response. I wonder how that question will be edited. The producer is not filmed asking the questions and, if he choses to, he could re-word them in an edit suite and cut my responses to suit. I realise sadly that I have been naïve. This programme might have been commissioned by an arts channel, but I have a sneaking suspicion our production company has Endemol-type aspirations for the show and that it is not the type of programme I thought I would be part of making.

I decide it is important I remind myself why I am here, despite the constantly changing circumstances around me. Even though I feel immense pressure right now (and not just from being wedged between a cello and an ice cream cabinet), I know I have to find a way to make this work. I want to leave this experience grinning like our Roman ticket vendor, not visibly depressed as this morning's breakfast waitress had been.

Right now, I think it's time to come out of hiding and find Johan and the crew.

I step out of the bar and am greeted by a beautiful sunset, which I stop to watch briefly before entering the village to find everyone. We decide to call it a wrap for the day and get some food. A lovely French lady serves us a simple but beautiful meal. We feast on local produce, grilled vegetables from the surrounding fields, and sample the local hand-made pasta called 'pici'. Despite the oral temptations on offer, the restaurant was empty, with everyone at the outdoor show in the square. I realised I could use power from the restaurant to use my amp and decided on an impromptu post-meal concert on the street, to coincide with people leaving the theatre show. I needed to play.

Strategically, it was not the best position as the exit to the show was on another street, but I played the best I had so far, venting the day's frustration through a number of improvised looped compositions. Despite the location, people came to listen and I even sold a couple of the *Painting with Music* CDs. It was a personal success and the crew's obvious delight meant a lot to me.

Consequently, the day finished on a high none of us had predicted and I felt proud to have made it happen. I felt that I had really discovered something about myself

– that through performance I had the ability to turn a situation around. The same time I started to learn to play the cello as a child, my Dad had become seriously ill with cancer. Strangely, I have little recollection of that time (or at least the bad parts of it) but I do remember playing for him and my mum and seeing how happy it made them during what must have been a painful and stressful time. I wonder if subconsciously the seed was sown then, that I became aware of the positive effect of being able to entertain.

The producer and I made peace and, despite a moment of panic losing Johan in the pitch dark walking back to the B&B (we found him eventually and have decided to arm him with a torch from now on), it felt like a positive end to a mentally challenging day.

Thursday 12th August DAY 13
– MONTICCHIELLO (TUSCANY) – FLORENCE

Waking up has become an exciting and surreal experience since beginning this journey, because almost every morning it is in a different location, another room that I could not have predicted the day before. At first I had found it unsettling, but now as the journey continues I have grown to enjoy the experience. Today was particularly nice, as the bed and breakfast located at the foothill of the town is lovely. It is a working farmhouse and my room had once been the owner's son's room. There are still toys in the corner, and the walls are adorned with his paintings of cartoon characters. It felt so homely and, as was happening frequently on this trip, I felt privileged to be inside someone else's home and life, to be getting a glimpse of their story and history.

With the idea of putting on a show suspended for the time being, the new plan was for Johan and me to go to a bigger town. We would head for Florence, where Johan could continue painting and looking for galleries, and I could try a new challenge – seeing if I could get my CD airplay on a local radio station.

I have always wanted to go to Florence. I have been there once, but since I drove straight out from the airport down to the Tuscan countryside, it doesn't really count. Another UNESCO world heritage site, Florence is considered by most to be the birthplace of the Renaissance. It is also known as the 'Athens of the Middle Ages', so it seems only right to include it on our journey.

Geographically, the distance from our village in Tuscany to Florence was short, but local trains with long delays made it a lengthy and tiring journey. I guess it is simply a matter of supply and demand that explains why local train journeys always seem unnecessarily arduous. In England I have also found it frequently frustrating that it can take so long to travel by train on lesser used routes, but at least I have found the Italian network to be fair priced and the trains large and airy. When they have been packed, the humour within the carriages never fails to cheer me up and I am delighted by the unusually convivial atmosphere where strangers chat and share food (and the occasional sneaky cigarette out of the connecting carriage windows). I realise sadly I have never encountered such an atmosphere on a UK train.

All the local radio stations were closed by the time we got there and Johan was also feeling frustrated. I decided to go on a reccie of the town to escape an escalating collective negativity similar to the one I had felt brewing yesterday during the day.

I found a little rock-themed bar called 'One-Eyed Jack' near one of the town's main bridges that reminded me of the smaller pubs I used to play as a teenager. I struck up conversation with the barman, initially to divert his attention from the fact I'd eaten all the crisps he'd put out on the bar for paying customers, but managed to secure the chance to play there that evening. The producer had suggested (no, told us) to check in to the same five-star hotel as the crew, so we now have only 90€ left. We may face a hostel tomorrow if I don't earn any money this evening.

I feel another surge of resentment towards the producer. We still have three weeks left and this journey is tough enough, what with the unpredictability, uncertainty and unfamiliarity we face on a daily basis, while still trying to be creative and engaged artists. But I know this feeling is unhealthy and decide not to let it linger. At least with the influence of the producer we are guaranteed to be permanently challenged...

My concert that evening at the rock bar is plagued by further amp problems, but I make 30€. It all helps.

Friday 13th August DAY 14
– FLORENCE, ITALY

Today did not start out well, despite the best efforts of a wonderfully abundant, ripe-for-the-picking breakfast spread. We had planned yesterday to return to the radio stations in the hope they would not be shut in the morning. (Local radio stations often pre-record shows for later broadcast and shut early.) But the producer had other plans: he wanted me to try and crash someone else's busking pitch in the town centre.

For me as an artist, this feels fundamentally wrong. Nor could I work out what could possibly be gained from my doing this. Belittling another artist by rocking up with a TV crew and playing over them? No, a flat no, and I would not be swayed on this one. But the producer was not taking no for an answer and, for the first time since the trip began, I felt truly miserable.

I thought about the choices I had made as a musician over the years in order to make a living. I did try busking once. As a teenager, accompanied by two friends and buoyed by our popularity jamming on the field next to our favourite watering hole on Wimbledon common, we had decided to 'go professional' outside the train station. My friends, Des and James, were dressed in their finest array of mismatched clothes, the latter proudly sporting a large black-brimmed gentleman's hat, me in a recently acquired denim waistcoat I had deemed sufficiently 'arty' for the occasion. Our little band had no sooner placed the brimmed hat on the ground and struck our first chord before being spotted by the local policeman. We made one pound ten pence and a boiled sweet (which I distinctly remember being of the strawberry-flavoured variety) before being asked to move on by our uniformed nemesis.

Though I definitely enjoyed more success in the proceeding years as a session musician, I often had to take part-time jobs in between music jobs, experiencing the curious sensation of living two lives which held almost no similarities. Both required the ability to appear professional and to work hard, but only one allowed me to indulge my passion. During my forays into the nine-to-five world I saw how miserable I would become in an office environment. Choosing to temp so I would still have the flexibility to take music jobs as and when they might occur. I wasn't scared of hard work but became sad surrounded too frequently by people who seemed to resent my other life which, despite my best efforts to conceal, I would have to explain when taking time off. (One bitter office manager even locked me in a filing cupboard for four hours once, afterwards claiming she had no idea I was in there despite her having asked me to go there in the first place.)

It wasn't all bad though. I also met wonderful, kind, curious people who enjoyed living vicariously through the tales they would ask me to tell on returning from one tour or another. One particular lady would often remind me not to give up on my dream of working on music full-time, and to enjoy the freedom from the regimented nine to five routine that my talent might provide. And so I felt particularly frustrated now. I had some time ago, through the signing of my publishing deal, achieved my status as a full-time musician and cherished the opportunity to work solely on something which I truly loved. But now, with the constant demands of participating on a TV show, I felt a total loss of freedom similar to that I had felt in the low lit basements of temping past. But this time it was much worse; it was a type of mental prison I was starting to feel trapped in because of my need to shut down and block out the unreasonable demands I felt were now being placed on me.

Finally I felt I was at a breaking point of sorts and I told the producer he could send me home. It is one thing to quit a challenge because you personally aren't strong enough, but it is another to go because you do not wish to fight anymore. I don't like conflict at the best of times: I'm more likely to walk away from a fight than engage in one and, at this point, I felt the line had been crossed into relentlessly bullying. I felt sick, I couldn't eat the breakfast. I went upstairs to my room and, for the first time since the Ex told me of his infidelity, I cried.

This time one month ago I had been looking forward to summer holidays with my boyfriend. In that ensuing four weeks, I had lost him and my home, and found myself stuck in a hotel in Florence with five people I barely knew, a performing puppet on a reality TV show. I'd also been told at breakfast that I wouldn't be allowed to do any more gigs after yesterday – it simply wasn't exciting enough to film. But, for me, that is the essence of the art of survival. When things get tough that is what I do, I play concerts and perform for people. I don't crash other people's busking pitches in busy piazzas.

The weather seemed to empathise with me, and we had the first proper rain since the trip began. Just as the arrival of rain-filled streets in previously sun-filled Italy surprised me, so did the producer's sudden change of tone towards me. After the morning interview to camera he, to give him his due, apologised. He said he had got like a dog with a bone. I saw a vulnerability in him then, and realised he really wasn't a bad person. We just had completely different agendas.

Dressed in ill-fitting water-proofs, which provided some necessary light-hearted teasing all round, we trudged our way through the centre of town and returned to the radio station closest to the hotel. It was open. Furthermore, the people at Radio Toscana were fantastically helpful.

Not only were they willing to play the CD on air but, after hearing the challenge, they suggested I do an interview on their live pre-lunch show. I could broadcast a request for help and see if any of the listeners responded. They even allowed Johan to set up his paints and canvas on their covered fifteenth century balcony so he could start his next large scale portrait.

Radio Toscana officially rocks.

For the first time on the trip I felt really quite nervous. I would have to do the interview in Italian and, while I can speak just enough to get by, it is quite another thing for me to attempt to express myself to the listeners of an Italian radio station. Somehow, maybe egged on by the contagious enthusiasm and excitement of my Italian radio hosts, I made it through the interview. Now we would have to wait and see if anyone responded.

I took this chance to spend some much-needed time alone, leaving the crew in the radio station and Johan painting furiously on the balcony. I went in search of solace in the famous *Piazza del Duomo*, which houses the magnificent *Basilica di Santa Maria del Fiore*. I find this piazza particularly interesting because, unlike most I have seen, the church in its enormity, almost swallows up the square. Nevertheless, it is beautiful. I sit on the curb. The sun has replaced the rain and quickly dries the cobblestones surrounding me. I wondered about Radio Toscana's listeners. Who tunes into that station on a Friday lunchtime? What might they offer us? Would we get *any* offers of help? My first ever media appeal. I was optimistic, a bit excited.

I returned to radio HQ where my questions were immediately answered. We had two offers: one from a local restaurant offering to feed us for free that night in exchange for a cello performance and one from a man living in Parma who was having a party for the Italian *ferragosto* holiday, which happened to be this weekend. We could stay the whole weekend with him if I play for the party.

We accept both offers instantly.

I feel an enormous sense of relief. This will make good filming, and the pressure will be off me to provide anything more than my art. At least until Monday, which will in days, be almost the halfway point on our journey. I realise I can do this. We will make it.

Johan's hard work is slowly giving way to another magnificent portrait. This time he is working from a photograph he took of our Stef. It is amazing to watch him work, totally consumed by the creative process, ignoring offers of food and drink. I decide to leave him to it. I totally understand, I have a similar way of being when I am in the middle of a composition. One of the radio presenters invites us to get some lunch so, minus Johan, we all follow him to a fantastic doorstep *piadina* (a sort of thin pizza sandwich) bar. His English is fantastic and he has a quirky, very 'British', accent which he explains to me came from wanting to learn to speak English after listening to The Beatles. He wanted to understand the lyrics and learnt his pronunciation from John Lennon's songs. This struck a particular chord (excuse the pun) with me, the idea that music could inspire someone enough to want to learn to communicate and understand a world outside of the one they were born in.

In fact, he loves the Beatles so much that his entire look, down to his glasses, is also evidently inspired by John Lennon; and he'd even sung in a Beatles tribute band when he was younger. I feel a little ashamed to admit that this display of fanaticism would ordinarily leave me feeling a bit uneasy, but this gentle, unassuming man had a beautiful, innocent passion which I found genuinely heart warming.

The evening ends up being another with a positive resolution. At his request, the producer and I had an early evening heart to heart on the rooftop balcony of the hotel. It was good to clear the air and, despite our being so frequently at odds, I do have a large amount of respect for him. I understand that being the creator of the show he also feels under an enormous amount of pressure, both to justify his choice of format for it and to realise this and produce a successful programme for his company.

It also reminds me that everyone on the team is, in some way, taking a personal challenge by being here. The crew also wake up each morning not knowing what might happen next or where we might end up. It is easy to forget, when the pressure is on, that while I am taking this journey I am also very much part of five other people's adventures and that, despite the different roles we have within this, we are also inevitably linked by this challenge. I have to respect the fact that things might be a bit weird sometimes. It's like going on holiday with a new boyfriend for the first time, but with five of them, for five weeks, and with no night-time romps to pacify the awkward moments that might occur during the day – or at least none I am intending to participate in!

So, air cleared, it's time for the free dinner offered to us by radio listener and restaurant owner of *Il Profetta* (The Prophet), Claudio. As soon as we arrive I know it will be a fantastic night. Claudio is so warm and friendly and ever so slightly over-excited. The crew are given a table outside, while Johan, cello and I are whisked into the narrow, busy, typically-Italian eatery. He doesn't seem at all bothered about me playing the cello, though (which is just as well as right now there is no room to set up and play amongst the diners). He is, however, very concerned to feed us as much food as it is humanly possible to eat.

The menu looks amazing, with lots of fresh fish and salads, and after so long eating scrounged carbohydrates from morning buffets I am excited at the prospect of a healthy meal. But our host has other plans. He wants to give us a special menu. And so begins an evening of gastronomic enormity the likes of which I have never and, with no disrespect to our wonderful host, ever hope to experience again. We work our way slowly and methodically through no less than five courses of food. And each course an apparent ode to cheese. I am not sure why exactly. Whatever the reason, for me this is mildly disastrous, as I am in fact allergic to a great many varieties of the yellow stuff. I sneak poor Johan as much as he can stomach on top of his own enormous portions. Eventually there is a pause in dishes arriving at our table. Phew, I think, it's over.

However, the pause proves only to be for dramatic purposes, necessary for the announcement of *Il Profetta's* piece de la resistance, the very same dish I am told proudly by our host, that John Travolta had eaten at the restaurant on a visit some years before... A giant, magnificent, bowl of...cheese! A bowl made of cheese containing a large amount of pasta combined with an even larger melted amount of my dairy nemesis.

It was hilarious, and while it did actually smell delicious, sadly for me it was completely inedible. Despite Johan's skin colouring, I truly think I could see him turning a little green. I will never think of John Travolta in the same way again. He is truly wasted as an actor if he has the skill to put away that entire dish.

The worst part was that Claudio was so absolutely lovely and so wanting to please. I glanced at the cello case next to me: if I was quick maybe I could just pour a little of the...no, this wasn't an option, I reluctantly conclude. So, instead, I see if pushing the cheese around, by means of deconstructing the outer shell of baked parmesan, might at least make it look like I'd eaten some. Achieving partial success, I manage to conceal the rest under a napkin I strategically position on top of the dish, praying only the kitchen dishwasher will discover my deception.

Johan and I got talking to the people on the table next to us. (They were probably wondering who in their right mind orders five courses of cheese but were too polite to actually ask.) The trio were father, mother and daughter from Australia, also travelling across Europe. They wanted to share an experience with their daughter before she had grown up and saw the world for herself. It was such a lovely idea and they were such great people. After hearing our story, they paid for Johan to do a portrait during their dinner and I was genuinely touched by their wishes of luck for us as they left – although in retrospect maybe they were referring to our ability to digest our dinner.

The meal ended many hours (and, I am guessing, an Italian national cheese shortage) later with chocolate made by Claudio's wife, which he proudly presented to us while patting his chest. I thought at first he had also had the *formaggio* finale and was suffering awful heartburn or worse, an imminent cheese-induced heart attack, until he asked us what we thought the secret of his happiness was, with apparently no shortage of breath. He proceeded to take a photo from his waistcoat breast pocket. It showed two smiling teenagers and he explained that it was a photo of him and his wife, aged fifteen. He tells me it was taken just after they met, and that they have been together ever since. This, he tells me, is the secret of happiness. I feel humbled by such a simple yet powerful statement and honoured that he has shared his personal philosophy with us. I am reminded of our taxi driver in Athens and wonder if there is a reason, given my current status, that I am being reminded of the power of love by these strangers I am encountering during this journey

The restaurant has emptied and he asks me if I will play a little cello for his wife. I gladly do. Warmed by the wine and the kindness of our hosts, I conclude it has been an incredibly special night.

Saturday 14th August DAY 15
– FLORENCE, ITALY – PARMA, ITALY

We woke this morning penniless. We'd spent our last euros on last night's hotel room and needed to make enough money to take the train. The camera-man suggested busking at a food market he'd visited on a previous visit to Florence. I love European food markets; the smells and colours, the way people stroll around tasting and talking. It's a completely different experience from walking around our modern, trolley-filled supermarkets. *Mercato Centrale* doesn't disappoint. Built in the nineteenth century, the two level building contains numerous stalls, selling fruits, vegetables, meats and flowers. It was also perfect as it gave us an escape from the continuing heavy rain.

On the lower level, next to a café, I decide to set up and play. A brief performance to the uninterested diners, most of whom appear to be foreign tourists, proves financially fruitless, but then we meet Sharon and her daughter. From San Franscico, they are staying in Bologna and decided to take a day trip into Florence. It's interesting that we have met more Americans with the cameras present than any other nationality. I don't think that they are particularly attracted by the possibility of being filmed, just that considering their televisually obsessed culture they are less scared of it. Whatever the reason, we were thankful they approached us as they bought a copy of the *Painting with Music* CD and commissioned a sketch portrait from Johan, which means we were able to afford the train fare to leave Florence. We learnt that Sharon's mother is an artist. They were sympathetic and excited by our challenge and also taking their own, learning Italian at a school in Bologna for the summer. They took photos of us and I thought about how strange it was that we would be featured in the evenings they shared with their friends when they eventually returned home to the States and recounted their holiday adventures. The world suddenly felt incredibly small.

We left the market and I felt ready to leave Florence, but the producer and Johan had been discussing a visit to the *Uffizi* art gallery. It turned out to be a stressful diversion, the queue was too long (a shame, as I would dearly have loved to have seen some of the artistic treasures it houses) and we abandoned aspirations of getting in just in time to make it to the station, in part thanks to a cab driver who clearly spent his youth hanging out with Valentino Rossi (the famous Italian motorcycle racer) – if I'm wrong, he should have.

Halfway through the two-hour journey between Florence and Parma, on our way to the home of our mystery host (I have since found out is called Nicola), for the *ferragosto* weekend, sitting on my suitcase in the corridor of another packed old Italian train, I make a quick phone call and let him know our time of arrival. It is amazing to think that in less than an hour our lives will collide.

We arrived at Parma train station exhausted from hauling our ever-increasing amount of luggage (Johan now also carrying the portrait he completed on Radio Toscana's balcony). It is frustrating that so few train stations have lifts, meaning we have to negotiate flights of platform-linking stairs. At least we have chosen to be laden with the baggage that is slowing our vertical progress. I think about how frustrating it must be for disabled people and how sad it is that in this day and age, with all our modern technology, we still give such little regard to the parts of our society that are in the minority.

The producer takes the chance to get a quick interview with us before we meet Nicola and we are asked to predict what we think he will be like. I have in fact spent the past hour thinking about this. I have never accepted a request to stay at a complete stranger's house before. I have also never offered my home to someone I didn't know. What sort of person calls in on a radio show and offers his home to two artists taking a crazy televised challenge across Europe? I had no idea. He hadn't sounded mad on the phone earlier, but then I'm not sure I would have been able to detect insanity in a two minute phone call with a man who spoke practically no English.

For the purposes of the interview, I decide he will be middle-aged; a family man who loves the arts and took some crazy trips in his youth, and so felt a certain empathy which fuelled his generous offer.

Nicola is, in fact, a twenty-five-year-old half Sicilian/ Italian, who turns up in his car with his best friend, grinning and excited. His father is on holiday, so he has the apartment they normally share to himself this weekend. In the brief time it takes for Johan and me to leave the crew and drive from the station to his home, I realise what a warm, open and friendly person he is and any fears I may have had are allayed.

His home is a typical suburban Italian flat in a block of around five storeys, each reached via a wide marble-floored staircase with wooden banisters. Smells of home cooking escaping from each large wooden-doored flat we walk past. Thankfully, with the absence of a lift and all our luggage, Nicola's own comfortably sized and incredibly homely abode is on the second floor. I have the small bedroom and am currently surrounded by 101 Dalmatians, or at least prints of them, on the bedspread. Johan is staying in our host's father's room and Nicola and his girlfriend Giovanna are in the other room, sleeping beneath name-plates made in the style of car number-plates. If I listen hard enough, I can just make out the scratching coming from the living room, the source of which is his seven-year-old pet rabbit, Sid, who has a particular fondness for Italian crackers. Everything about the place is warm and friendly. Yet again strangers have opened up their home and their hearts to us and I feel suitably humbled.

The producer has decided that since we have the whole weekend here, we should have this first night off from filming. I thought this was a nice gesture – if a little at odds with his habitual aspiration for good television over personal consideration. He is aware what an act of generosity Nicola's invite is, and doesn't want to abuse this with intruding into his life with a camera, or at least not just yet. After a short tour of Parma, including an *aperitivo* pitstop at a lovely little bar in the centre of town, we go to Nicola's friend's restaurant in the countryside for dinner, where the crew plan to join us for their evening off.

The large country restaurant was almost empty apart from us. Actually, after half-an-hour it was completely empty apart from our table, which made me feel particularly bad, as a fellow performer, for the hired entertainment, who turned out to be a friend of Nicola's. Providing renditions of everything from Elvis Presley (dance moves included) to Shania Twain, aided by his digital backing tracks, Beppe turned out to be a one-man entertainment powerhouse.

Buoyed by a generous sampling of the local wine, and without the pressure of having to work, crew and team JJ were thrown a chance to bond a little more. Without too much arm-twisting the camera-man and I were persuaded to relieve Beppe temporarily with our version of *Hey Jude*. The crowd went wild (oops, I already mentioned ours was the only table occupied in the building, didn't I?) and we decided to allow Beppe a little extra wine-sampling time by also attempting our version of *The Living Daylights*, accompanied by some James Bond-inspired dance moves – which I can only say I am happy to have been doing with the cameraman, since it meant that it couldn't be filmed.

Sunday 15ᵗʰ August DAY 16
– PARMA, ITALY

Johan is painting on Nicola's little balcony and I have just done the first washing of the trip, after Nicola lent us his washing machine. (I suspect less through generosity and more through disgust that we were walking around in oil paint-stained, dust-covered and, dare I say it, smelly clothes.) The TV crew are due to arrive to film in half-an-hour and I am reveling in this brief moment of domestic normality.

The sunshine has returned but I can feel we are further north. It is slightly chillier, but still glorious compared to the average UK summer. The plan today is to go to Nicola's grandfather's house in the countryside for the *ferragosto* party.

The Roman Empire originally celebrated on this day to honour the gods, specifically Diana and the cycle of fertility. The name of the festival derives from the original Latin, *Feriae Augusti* (Holiday of the Emperor Augustus). Nicola's countryside house proves a fitting place to celebrate an Emperor's holiday. It is beautiful. The original house is huge and now disused, his grandparents preferring to live in a smaller house in the grounds next door.

This doesn't stop Nicola showing us around it, though, and it is truly amazing. It seems his grandparents didn't move anything from the moment they left the main house, and it is a perfectly preserved time capsule with original furniture and furnishings untouched since the 1960s. It is incredible to see and also a little spooky. There is still a plate in one of the sinks, as if someone has just finished washing up and nipped off to find a tea towel to do the drying. The attic is full of original copies of the Italian national newspaper, *Corriere della Sera* – I see one dated 1915. Nicola's great-grandparents had been wealthy landowners and he explained that the bell on the top of the main house would have been used to call all the village workers to the house in the morning.

The house is surrounded by vineyards and they still produce a little of their own wine. Nicola gives us some to sample, for which he is scolded by his grandfather later. He had opened the wrong bottle and we had taken a large slug of the home-made vinegar, which I was relieved to hear as this is exactly how it had tasted, though my thoroughly English politeness didn't let on at the time. They also had fig trees from which I tasted the sweetest, most beautiful fruit I've ever had.

In view of the perfect weather, we decide to dine *al fresco* and a long trestle table is set up in the courtyard.

Johan and I sit and eat with Nicola plus five of his friends, our crew and, a little later, our karaoke Elvis impersonator, the one and only Beppe.

Later I set up and played a few numbers in the shade of the family's disused garage opposite our outdoor dining table, but it was Beppe and his duets with Stef that really stole the show. The crew were intermittently shooting parts of the day's escapades, but it felt relaxed enough to almost be a day off and it was only on the production of release forms for Beppe and Nicola's friends that I remember this is also work. Beppe is instantly worried: he is contracted to be on an Italian talent show on television later in the year and is worried this will conflict with the strict rules of engagement of his other contract.

It's another frustrating reminder of the increasingly controlling and manipulative way show business works. It seems to me slightly ridiculous that this talented young singer is restricted in the things he can do in advance of even appearing on this talent show, on which he has no guarantee he will even be successful.

After much discussion, it was agreed Beppe would not sign the form and would be cut from any footage he might otherwise have appeared in – which was a shame because, trust me, you would have enjoyed watching him. I truly hope his gamble to stay exclusive to the Italian TV talent show paid off and that as you are reading this, he is in fact a huge, international hip-wiggling, Elvis-impersonating TV star. But the sad truth is, he probably isn't.

In the evening we head back to downtown Parma,

which is as sleepy as you'd expect a small town to be on a national holiday. But, as is becoming increasingly evident and typical of Nicola's giving personality, he is thinking of us and how we can make some money to get to our next destination.

He has arranged a concert for me in the little bar we went to on the first evening we arrived and where I had found out he a) used to be a pole dancer in a nightclub and b) once had a Rottweiler called Shakira (I couldn't think of a better animal to name after her myself). Though we had spent little more than thirty minutes there before, as seems to be typical of Italians, they greeted us like old friends.

The bar wasn't busy but the evening was warm so I set up outside and played a set which, despite the now habitual technical limitations, went well. I ended up making an extraordinary 105€, mainly thanks to the generosity of the bar owner and staff who paid me for playing, and some sales of *Painting with Music*. Later, back at Nicola's over a cup of tea, he tells me how relieved he is that he was able to help us and that he would gladly have paid for our train tickets to Milan – our next planned destination – if we hadn't made any money.

I go to my room and find a little panda propped on my pillow and glance to a picture on the bedside table of his brother as a child holding the same toy. I am touched by such consideration, as inexpensive as it may be, this is a little family heirloom and so on one level priceless, and yet Nicola's desire to make his guests welcome is such that he is willing to entrust me with this, hoping it might make me feel more at home. Such a sweet gesture, and yet again I can't believe our luck at meeting him.

Monday 16th August DAY 17
– MILAN, ITALY

We are on our way from Parma to Milan. We left a clearly emotional Nicola (who insisted on paying our train fares anyway) and a clearly relieved Giovanna (who had seemed perpetually bemused by the temporary additions to her boyfriend's social circle). The producer has deemed the fares not to count as help from friends as we did not know them before the trip and have exchanged skills during our stay.

Johan seems a bit out of sorts and I resolve to look after him today. I know that he has found the past couple of days tough. Although my Italian is poor, it is still good enough to get by, and with practically no-one we met over the weekend speaking any English I think he felt a bit excluded, despite my best efforts to translate.

I understand how he feels. I lived in Copenhagen in Denmark for over a year when I had my last record deal. While the major difference was that almost all Danes speak perfect English, I could still empathise with how Johan felt because in social circles, once I had joined them, people soon forgot I couldn't understand Danish. This was flattering in as much as it meant I was one of the gang, but it also meant I would often spend whole evenings not having a clue what was going on, and subsequently joining in a little too enthusiastically with the consumption of *Snapps* so that it mattered less.

Johan reveals to me today that he thinks the producer and crew see me as some sort of leader. I instantly feel complimented, but am also very surprised. I have spent a large part of the trip so far dogged by self-doubt, but realise that my perception of the situation is inevitably completely different from everyone else's. When I think about it, I realise I have had a tendency on this trip to take control of situations if I thought they seemed to be evolving into something counter-productive. For example, making sure to try and do some research at internet cafés for our next destination and looking after Johan's share of the money. But the latter was at Johan's request and with the former, I just thought it prudent given our situation. I have a rare moment of wondering how I will be perceived on TV by the audience, but quickly try to change my train of thought as I know it isn't helpful to think about this. I turn instead to hoping we are lucky in Milan today. Nicola has just sent a text; he already misses us and says we will stay in his heart.

Arriving in Milan, we plan to go to art galleries to try and sell some more of Johan's work. His portrait of Stef is now finished, thanks to an extra few hours in the sunshine working on Nicola's balcony. But first we need to find out where to go, so I head straight to an internet café to research possibilities. I realise how much I am enjoying this element of the challenge. Researching and planning is not something Johan has any interest in, but I'm not at all bothered by this (everyone has their strengths and weaknesses) and any frustration I might have felt about Johan's reliance on me arranging everything is negated by the feeling of pride I have in successfully locating something. Maybe Johan is right, maybe I am a bit of a leader. It is not something that is easy to discover working in the way that I normally do as a musician.

However, my joy at finding suitable galleries was short lived, as it became apparent that everywhere in Milan was closed. We had assumed that *ferragosto* had finished, but the holiday is extended for the business community over into the following Monday. It was also becoming increasingly evident from brief glances at hotel tariffs that the money we had would not get us a room here. I started to think that good fortune had spoilt us a little. After such an incredible few days of random generosity from the people of Florence and Parma, the hostility of a large, industrial, money-orientated city was a shock. The producer and Johan both seemed convinced that trying to blag a hotel room for free was a great idea. I didn't feel comfortable with this, as simply getting something for free wasn't really part of the challenge. I realise that in order to make 'better TV', the entire purpose of the show is often compromised at the whim of the producer, but also, confusingly, reinforced by him if the situation suits. The rules and boundaries in the game shift, making it impossible to play correctly.

I decide resistance is futile and that the only way to deal with the situation is to join in with enthusiasm, so we embark on a vaguely humiliating and fruitless round of cold calling five star hotels and explaining our mission.

Each perfectly air-conditioned, designer-furnished lobby we entered greeted us with vague amusement. And after a nondescript amount of waiting time, (during which we would peruse the varying snack menus, salivating over descriptions of obscenely over-priced dishes, while mentally moving into our ensuite king-sized rooms, complete with more pillows than an Ikea showroom), we would be woken from our revelries with the curious mathematical equation of waiting time for response = Politeness / Dishonesty:

Example 1: (after 20 minutes of lobby observation) 'We'd love to but just realised we are full booked!' Politeness 10 Honesty 0

Example 2: (after 10 minutes of waiting) 'If you come back next month we might be able to sort something out with head office.' NEXT MONTH! Dear god, we just explained we are here for two days... Politeness 7 Honesty 3

Example 3: (after 30 seconds of entering the building) 'Please leave the building with your camera crew.' Politeness 0 Honesty 10

After the fifth or sixth futile attempt and an equally fruitless busking session in the main square, we were hot and tired. We left the crew dining at some beautiful Milanese restaurant and retreated to the anonymity of the McDonald's opposite the main train station. This was a particularly low moment for me, being in a country synonymous with some of the best cuisine in the world, and finding myself picking at a one euro fillet-o-fish burger. I was also left with a mouth that felt a little like I had some sort of fur ball, similar to those cats cough up, stuck there as a lingering reminder of the chips. The only good thing was that the Italian McDonald's, unlike its British counterpart, sold cheap beer. We decided to treat ourselves.

Buoyed by our current state of malnutrition, humiliation and slight inebriation, we decided to try the hotel opposite the station for a room. They had one. We couldn't afford it, but we weren't obscenely far off. I asked the manager if we could pay half now and half when we got back from the cash machine and a stroll around town. This was, of course, a little white lie. We didn't have credit cards but we were running out of options. It was a huge risk – we would lose the money we were giving him now (every penny we currently had) if we didn't return with the rest later. But, lie undetected, we got our room. Now we just had to find a way to pay for it.

The hotelier had recommended an area called *Porta Genova*, a district of Milan named after the city gate of the old Spanish Walls and on a canal (the *Naviglio*), for our 'evening out'. In the darkness, the canal was lit by strings of fairy lights with restaurants and bars lining either side of the bank. We didn't find *Vicolo Lavandaie,* a small street where the Milanese women used to wash their clothes in the *Naviglio's* waters, but I did spot a little restaurant which, for some reason,

I was instantly drawn to. I have started to trust my instincts in a way I never would have done before this trip. Nothing is guaranteed, despite my best efforts with sporadic internet café research visits, and when you have no definite income or notion of what will come next, you have to start trusting in yourself in a way you might not normally.

And it seems that when you give it the chance, the old gut feeling is often spot on. We are greeted by a friendly young man, ridiculously good looking, (in the kind of effortless movie star way most Milanese men are) who, on hearing of our challenge, introduces us to the owner. I have realised the only way to guarantee an income is to ask a fee for entertaining, in the way I would do if I was working as a singer in a London bar or restaurant, of which I have some previous experience as a jazz singer with backing tracks when I was younger. Luckily for me, the owner is sympathetic; he used to own a vinyl pressing plant – also his Labrador, Ariel, has taken a liking to me, a good sign apparently. If the crowd like me, he will pay me an unspecified amount.

The producer and crew decide they will also dine there before I play. I am ridiculously thankful, suspecting this might help encourage the owner's generosity towards us at the end of the night. It does, we sell a CD to a table of diners after my concert, and he pays me 100€ and gives Johan and me drinks on the house. Saved again, we style out our arrival at the hotel as if there had never been an issue with paying, and hope tomorrow the bank holiday will be over. Business as usual might lead us to a little luck.

Tuesday 17th August DAY 18
– MILAN, ITALY

Today we officially reach the halfway point of the challenge. Sadly, though, given our current state of frustration, we have no desire to celebrate this. Milan, it would appear, is not closed for a bank holiday – instead, pretty much everything is closed for the whole of August. It is a veritable ghost town. This is not good. Relying on my research, we walk from gallery to gallery in the hope that some other starving artists and dealers might be ignoring this month-long holiday, but it seems they too are all on the Italian coast somewhere, sipping cold *granita* and converting fake tans to real, while consuming large *gelato* purchased with their winter profits.

Our continued lack of funds means we have spent the day dragging around all our gear in the midsummer Italian heat, surviving on discarded biscuits from outdoor café tables (wrapped, I draw the line at half-eaten ones) and dry rolls I managed to take from this morning's breakfast buffet – which I feel I have no right to complain about the quality of.

I am amazed at my body's capacity to deal with the demands this challenge has placed upon it. I have written quite a lot about the psychological strains, but physically this journey is also tough because of the amount we are carrying between us, unaided. During the first week my rucksack straps cut into my shoulders so painfully I had to wedge a scarf I had brought with me under them to ease the pain. But I can now feel my muscles have become stronger and the skin on my shoulders has toughened to the point where I feel almost no discomfort. I have also now become accustomed to negotiating steep staircases and narrow spaces lifting both cello and suitcase.

There are other positive benefits. I feel generally fitter. I no longer burn in the sun. My skin glows with an even tan and frequent bouts of undernourishment have given me a flat stomach I haven't had (nor thought I would have again) since my early twenties. My new concern is remembering to wear a belt so as not to expose too much behind in my now loose fitting trousers, lest I provide a little too much amusement for the camera-man and potentially put viewers off their dinner when the programme is aired.

Back in the centre of Milan, sitting alone in the sunshine on a stone wall in a small piazza opposite *La Scala*, arguably one of the leading opera houses in the world, I really feel I should be enjoying this moment, but can't, such is the depth of my frustration and exhaustion. I tried to busk here earlier, but the *Polizia* swiftly put an end to that.

I have resorted to my standoffish London attitude of suspicion to strangers, fuelled by my disappointment at not fulfilling expectations of success in Milan. I feel guilty now that I had been so nonchalant with the young, down-on-his-luck translator/teacher who had joined me here earlier on his bicycle. He had clearly been depressed and I hadn't wanted that energy around me (with Johan also being frustrated and down). But now I feel bad – haven't I learnt anything about unconditional kindness from this journey?

I have a good friend called Luca who I work with in

A Real Journey

First night's accommodation

Team JJ

My Corfu gig

Creating *Painting with Music*
in Piazza Navona

Janie Price

Our cd production line
in Rome

Florentine philosophy

Doing our washing in Italy

Decorating the cello case

A Real Journey

Filming in Tuscany

Captain Jan's cargo ship

Our Edinburgh angel Jo

Radio Toscana rocks!

A Real Journey

Payment in Parma

Johan's portrait of me

The final ticket!

Travel weary feet (mine!)

The time capsule house
loft find

The final venue (the Roxy
in Edinburgh)

"Come on, Feijenoord!"

Payment for my Basel concert

A Real Journey

Johan before the unfortunate hair incident
in Amsterdam

Taking shelter in the Zürich kebab shop

Janie Price

The age of chivalry is dead!
(Zürich train station)

Nicola's ferragosto party in Parma

'real life' through my publishing company, co-writing songs. He lives near Milan and I decide to call him to hear a friendly voice. He doesn't understand why he can't help when I tell him how the challenge is going. I explain we will be disqualified and sent home if we receive help from friends, but this doesn't stop him discussing an elaborate plan to drive to Milan in various inventive disguises and randomly pass by my busking spot donating euros. If nothing else, his enthusiasm makes me chuckle, but I really don't think he understands when I tell him I have to go – I have biscuits to steal – and no, he really can't help.

I am also worried about Johan. He is a sensitive soul and easily demotivated, and he takes the tough days particularly hard. But this time I also feel drained, and unable to provide the necessary extra ten percent that would enthuse him again. To be honest, this time I really need him. It's become clear today that busking is fruitless, strict policing and the general lack of attention paid to us by the few tourists who also had no idea Milan closes for August, means I am panicking about trying to earn a crust. But a portrait or two from Johan might just get us the train fare out of here, which seems like a sound strategic move right now. I also feel guilty that my motivation to cheer him up is survival-driven. I have a sudden flash of memory of the film 'Alive'. I feel like one of the surviving passengers, trying to take a metaphorical bite out of Johan's frozen bottom in order to avoid my own starvation, and I already know it won't taste good.

I'm saved from my daydream of twisted fuselage and

night of the living dead style dining by a sudden and unpredictable improvement in Johan's state. (Goodness, maybe he's telepathic.) He leaps into action, trying to sell our CDs to passers-by in the nearby *Galleria Vittorio Emanuele II*. One of the things I have come to admire in Johan is his fearlessness around complete strangers. Of all the places to regain his mojo he has chosen the home of *haute couture* and meeting place of the great and (allegedly) good of Milan. Even the architecture here has a formidable history, its iron structure inspiring the Eiffel Tower in Paris. However, I also know that this fearlessness without guidance could land him in hot water, which it very nearly does as he attempts to sell a portrait and CD to two local policeman patrolling the *galleria*, who luckily (maybe they have seen the cameras) see the funny side and just move us on. Still, thanks to Johan's remarkable capacity for charming the general public, we do manage to make enough money from selling CDs to scrape together the necessary train fare to get us out of there.

It's time for a change of country – Johan and I (or is it just me taking a leadership role again?) decide the easiest way to continue northwards, and therefore in the direction of the desired end destination, is to travel up to Switzerland and onwards from there. There are frequent direct trains from Milan to Zurich, so we decide to head there next.

So, I'm writing this now from another train, which left the grand *Milano Centrale* station half-an-hour ago. Earlier, I managed to squeeze in another internet café research session and have found a couple of galleries in

Zurich that have confirmed they will be...OPEN! It's a positive prospect and provides optimism which is necessary, as after paying our train fare we now sit here with very little money; we're pretty sure not enough for accommodation. It is either very brave or completely ridiculous to be doing this, but after so many days of unpredictability the unknown carries less risk, somehow, than being knowingly static in a big city. We need to keep travelling and we need to find ways to create new opportunities. With this in mind, we felt we had little choice but to spend our money on this train and hope for the best in Switzerland.

We have a plan at least: we will hit the galleries I have researched tomorrow. We have no idea what will happen tonight, but travelling through the mountains feasting on leftover crisps, it feels like a good start. Johan is currently sketching a portrait for a young Swiss guy, who was sympathetic to our cause because his girlfriend is a cellist. It won't be enough to get us a room but it is a start.

Weirdly, for a self-confessed sun-worshipper, it also feels good to be travelling north. Geographically we are succeeding and progressing well, within the rules and with enough time. I think we will be ok financially, too, as long as we can just keep going.

The crew are also on the train with us. I realise it's nice to spend time with them again and I think, on some level, I can pretend we're just a group of mates travelling, on an adventure, and am able to suspend the reality of the situation – that we are taking a challenge, that I'm also a subject for television. They told me earlier that I should work on television, and should consider being a presenter. Oddly, I do understand what they mean. I enjoy talking to the camera and imagining how many people might connect and vicariously take the journey with us. I have the same feeling and yearning to connect when I write music and perform. Maybe at some point in the future, fate will intervene, as it did with my getting the opportunity to take this journey. These thoughts comfort and enthuse me, offering a necessary distraction from the producer's musings on Switzerland. He's telling us how he's always had a negative time there and thinks it will be tough. I hope he's wrong.

Wednesday 18ᵗʰ August DAY 19 – ZURICH, SWITZERLAND

It's 4.50am.

I am sitting on another stone bench but the view has changed. No sunshine, no grand late eighteenth century opera house to admire. Instead, I have two pairs of woolly-socked feet (Johan's and the producer's) pervading an odour I shall choose not to describe in case you happen to be eating while reading this.

I'm in Zurich train station for the second time in less than twelve hours. Our train from Milan was delayed en route and we didn't arrive in Switzerland until midnight, a tactical blow when we needed to make money in order to find somewhere to stay.

We launched ourselves into the bar and hotel-laden district near the station, which was heaving with drunken revellers. It was late but we were still optimistic. But positivity slowly gave way to mild horror as we discovered all the places cheap enough for our meagre budget were fully booked, and that none of the ones that weren't were going to take pity on us and offer discounted accommodation, even with (or possibly because) of our glamorous entourage.

We walked around for three hours, me snacking on our last remaining stash of various makes and shapes of biscuits we had 'found' in Italian hotel breakfast buffets and on outdoor café tables. Johan declined to eat even this, such was his distress at the possibility that we might actually have to sleep rough for the first time on our journey.

His fearlessness in trying to coax people into helping suddenly felt tiresome, irritating and, given the general levels of inebriation, irresponsible and even a little dangerous. The producer's pessimism on the train now seemed wholly justified. In addition, it was colder than Milan and it was raining. Soaked and clinging to all my belongings, I stopped a cab driver, hoping to get some advice on where might be a good place to go, but was met only with a steely glare and the information that without money we should prepare to sleep on the streets. It had the curious effect of making me feel about five-years-old, being sick after eating too much chocolate and finding little sympathy from my parents (although, to be fair, they were covered in the consequent fruits of my over-eating efforts, an extraordinary amount of brown, sticky, regurgitated goo).

I thought wistfully of Italy and its friendly inhabitants. I tried to imagine the same scenario there and concluded there was no way someone would not have tried to help us. Here, we were either greeted with mild amusement or disgust, and no genuine offers of help. But we had chosen to take this challenge – we couldn't just expect people to help us based on previous experience.

All through this damp desperate struggle, the cameras pursued and filmed us. Despite the added protection I should have felt from having them with us, I was starting to resent their presence at this point. I didn't want to be filmed going though this struggle, although I realised it was their job, their right in fact, to be doing so. At one point I actually hid in a dark doorway, eating my last acquired *Tuc* biscuit, just to get some rest from them following me.

As the bars closed and the drunks finally started to dwindle in numbers, we found a kebab shop which was still open and decided to take shelter from the rain and get warm. It's funny how the places I would normally never dream of going were the ones providing refuge when we needed it most. Johan managed to find the last of 'the living drunks', wandering zombie-like towards the warmth and light of our greasy sanctuary. A group of fellow Englishmen, they offered us to sleep in the corridor of their hotel. In addition to the fact the offer was not theirs to make (I was fairly sure the hotel manager wouldn't see the funny side of the situation the next day), I also felt distinctly uneasy around them. I had a rare flash of anger towards Johan for putting me in this situation. I understood his fear at sleeping rough, but likewise, entering an unknown guesthouse with five drunken men and only Johan for protection was not an option for me.

It was time for the crew to go to the hotel they had pre-booked, but the show's insurance requirements meant the producer had to stay with us should we have to sleep rough. So he, Johan and I sat with coffee purchased with the very last of our money until we were thrown out of the kebab shop when it shut at 4am.

We walked through the wet streets, hoping to stumble across some warm, brilliant late-night drinking den where we could take refuge. At this point I was actually most surprised at my lack of tiredness. With no proper food to sustain us and walking with all the gear all night, I should have felt exhausted, but I guess the adrenalin was keeping me alert. I felt quite animal-like, feral, hunting for shelter and knowing I mustn't rest. I could almost here the David Attenborough voiceover:

'And here we see two of the lesser spotted intrepid travellers, a rare sighting as this species is also crossed with the reality TV breed. Extraordinary to watch these creatures' behavior under pressure – the female's eyes slightly red and belly distended, we assume from eating food stuffs she would not normally harvest, the male's head down, as he has failed in his role as the hunter gatherer. Both traversing unknown terrain with their homes on their backs, it can be only a matter of time before they become prey to the indigenous species of the area...'

In the absence of any 'friendly inns for the night', we decided to head for the station, which had previously been closed. Luck of some sort was with us, as it had just opened and so, for the past fifty minutes, it is where I have been sitting, watching the world wake up. The producer is next to me, hunched up and nodding off intermittently. Johan is also next to me, prostrate, asleep on the wide stone bench. Deciding that the eighteenth century Irish writer, Edmund Burke, had in fact been correct when he said *'the age of chivalry is gone'*, it was clearly now up to me to stay awake and guard our belongings from the steady stream of drug addicts and drunks circling shark-like around our current position. I try to distract myself by painting my nails with the bright red nail polish I brought as my 'luxury item'. I find the futility of this activity, given our current circumstance, strangely comforting.

I refuse to feel miserable about our predicament though, happy that Johan has calmed down enough to get some rest. If I really think about it, I am mildly relieved: this should keep the producer's hot pursuit for TV gold at bay (if for no other reason than he may well be too exhausted tomorrow to insist on us doing anything too crazy); and this is a real challenge. Isn't that what I came here for? The key, glaring difference, of course, is that unlike the other poor souls wandering around here, for me, this experience is only temporary – or at least I hope it is.

Watching the people starting to clean the station, as a nearby bell chimes five o'clock, I think about how lucky I am in general. I think about the two Turkish men who ran the kebab shop we were in earlier, who spend at least six nights a week dealing with drunk, and I'm sure occasionally abusive, people until the small hours. And then they have to clean before they can even think about getting home, so I'm guessing the possibility of sleep is not even a vague reality until five or so in the morning. Then there are the street cleaners we saw on our nocturnal walk to the station, hauling heavy bins over their shoulders in the rain, and the man I can see now, scrubbing large grills down in preparation for making the early morning commuter snacks in the train station Burger King; tough, unsociable work and I'm guessing for little financial reward.

It is not that I am normally blinkered and unaware that other people have tough lives. But for the first time I am in a situation where I feel I can empathise. A true need for survival supercedes everything else. So far we have only had to experience this feeling once, but there are so many people for whom this is a way of life; a life with no small luxuries, no going to the pub with friends, no choosing a nice restaurant for dinner, no being tired from work and treating yourself to a night at the cinema –these options just don't exist.

Despite our challenging start in Zurich and my current sleep-deprived, malnourished state, I feel optimistic about today; after all, we are in one of the major cities for art in Europe. We know the galleries are open today and that Johan has a fairly high success rate for selling work. He has some good pieces with him, and we only need one sale to get us out of this situation. I can find somewhere to busk and we can try to sell some of our dwindling supply of *Painting with Music* CDs.

I also realise that while optimism is key to survival, it is also important to acknowledge your true state and how it is affecting you, in the hope you can adjust and make yourself an even stronger candidate for survival. Suddenly I'm thinking back to our last morning in Milan where I had had a weird moment. Bleary-eyed and still half asleep, the tiling in the hotel bathroom was almost exactly the same as that in the bathroom I had in the flat I had shared with the Ex. I had stretched the wrong way for the toilet roll in a moment of confusion and almost launched myself off the loo onto the floor, forgetting I was in fact in a hotel room and not there. I was struck by the newness of my situation and the knowledge that I would never go back to the little home I had made. I had felt suddenly and unpredictably sad.

I haven't been allowing myself to dwell on everything that happened before I began this journey. It would be pointless and self-harming to court the memories. But now I was starting to allow myself to ask, 'What comes next?' Sitting here on a stone bench, with two relative strangers my only source of solace and protection, sleeping rough in an unfamiliar town in central Europe with no money, no food and no guarantee when I might have any – the only guarantee that soon a camera crew would turn up and film my sorry state for a television audience – well, it's bound to make you wonder.

The truth is, I feel entirely average. I am not tall, not short, not stunning, not ugly. I am talented in some things and not in others. I have a £20,000 student

debt and a guilty secret that I occasionally read *Hello!*
Magazine in the hairdressers (I would like to stress,
however, that I would never sink to the murky depths
of actually buying it).

I realise, sadly, that as a product of this image-obsessed
world in which success and happiness are measured in
such bizarre, disproportionate and often damaging
ways, I can't quite get my head around the idea of being
average – which should be a wonderful thing when you
think about it. I am in fairly good health, despite my
debt I can afford to eat and drink, and I have friends and
family close to me. But I start to wonder if I will ever
fall in love with anyone again, if anyone will ever feel
the same way about me. When this journey ends I have
no home of my own to go back to. Where will I go? I'm
getting a bit emotional, I must be tired.

It's 5.35am now. The ticket office opened five
minutes ago, the guard keeping a small group of tired
tourists waiting until the exact second the big Swiss
clock in the station hit 5.30. I am starting to feel very
cold. It must be a combination of exhaustion and the
opening of more of the station entrance doors at the
other end of the concourse. In front of me is a small
kiosk producing smells I would normally not even
notice, walking by in a London station, but here they
smell like the first day of spring; beautiful, tempting
me, coffee and hot pastries.

I distract myself by taking pictures of Johan and
the producer, now both fast asleep on the stone
bench. I giggle to myself as I think about sharing
this photographic evidence with the rest of the crew

later this morning. I can feel myself getting more and more tired and decide I need another distraction. I dig around in my rucksack and find some colour marker pens. I decide to decorate my cello case; maybe I can make my own work of art to exhibit at the final show in Edinburgh?

I've just received a delayed text message from Stef (also now fondly nicknamed Nigel Man for her bloke-like ability to bond and communicate with the rest of the all male crew and unlikely strength considering her tiny build). It read:

Hey lovely. Hope you are warm and safe and in good company. My thoughts are with you guys and fingers and toes crossed that tomorrow is a wonderful and successful day for you both. Much love to you two X Sent 3:48

I think about how we have grown to be such a close team, despite our very different roles and aims, and realise how our current plight affects them too.

It's 7am now. Still awake, my cello case duly decorated in the manner of a crazed, wide-eyed, sleep-deprived traveller. I had decided on a selection of multi-coloured cartoon figures with speech bubbles encasing phrases that have become team sayings. It's a funny quirk of human nature that when a group spends any length of time together a sort of code language develops around jokes and shared experiences. Ours include:

'Pronto!' (The camera-man does a highly amusing, high-

pitched version of this Italian word, which we heard so
often when people were answering their phones there.)

'Save it for camera.' (Often said by the producer to me or
Johan when we are talking and he deems the discussion
important for inclusion on the show.)

'Your problem is you've got too much money.' (The
producer again, though I'm guessing he won't dare say
this for a few days now...)

'There's no such thing as a bad animal print combo.'
(Stef and I – if anyone from Vogue is reading this, you
can have that one for free.)

'You can't sleep here.' (OK, a new one from the Swiss
train station guard.)

'*Danke für nicht.*' (Also a new one: the producer's dry
response to our Swiss friend.)

'It's all got a bit Swiss.' (I'll be introducing that one later
today. A rough (London) translation would be: 'It's all
gone a bit Pete Tong.')

I'm celebrating the arrival of morning proper with a
long-life, pre-packed apricot jam-filled croissant (at least
I'm guessing that's what it's supposed to be as the object
I am holding doesn't in the least resemble the picture on
the packaging) that I had discovered earlier buried at
the bottom of my rucksack while I was looking for the

coloured pens.

I wonder if the producer may well be right about Switzerland. I was hoping to dispel his prejudice as myth, but with little success given our experience to date. I hadn't had much previous experience with the country either, excluding numerous painful experiences with their most famous culinary export, the Toblerone.

Maybe I should have considered this an early warning sign. What sort of country invents a chocolate bar which is designed purely to destroy the upper roof of your mouth? If you know a way to eat this crocodile toothed bar without the consequent need for open mouth surgery, please let me know.

Eventually, as the station fills with people, we are kicked off our stone slab. We seek refuge in a waiting room downstairs. With my trusty minders now awake, I collapse in the corner on the floor and get one-and-a-half-hour's blissful sleep, before I am woken by a guard who says I may not rest or even wait here (in the WAITING room).

Although it is now 10am, we still have to wait for the crew. So we have gone to the only other place we can afford, the golden arches of McDonald's. We spend the last of the small emergency change we have on a coffee to avoid being thrown out (it is still raining and chilly, so outdoors is not an option with this much equipment). I feel a bit irritated that we have to wait for the crew and spend our emergency pennies doing so. If this was truly the art of survival, Johan and I would already be on our way to the first gallery by now, but we are not allowed to go without the camera in case something 'exciting' happens. I'm also starting to feel nervous. If Johan sells one of the paintings, we are sorted. If he doesn't, we are in serious trouble. There is absolutely no way of knowing what will happen. I have just snuck to the toilet to get changed (from one set of dirty clothes to another); we have eaten nothing but rubbish for two days; we've had no sleep (save my neck-breaking cat nap) for twenty-six hours; and are carrying all our belongings. This is definitely a low point.

I try to comfort myself with the definites: Johan has sold three paintings so far. None for less than 499€. One for 2000€. It is possible. The variables: we are in a different country from the ones where we had success and, while Switzerland neighbours Italy, I have little evidence to suggest there is any cultural similarity. It is therefore entirely possible they will not respond in the same way to Johan's work, my playing or the fact we are also making a television programme.

It would appear Lady Luck has definitely left the building, this country and our lives. We spent the entire day, eight hours, walking from gallery to gallery. I have no idea quite how many kilometres we covered, carrying all our baggage unaided, undernourished and tired, but it was definitely too many. The worst responses were not the flat No's to Johan's work, but the Maybe's, the false hope provided by people just too gutless to be honest and point blank refuse to buy it. Johan wanted my support today going around the galleries, which I was happy to offer, so busking was abandoned in the hope of getting an instantly greater injection of cash by making an artwork sale. But watching Johan being repeatedly rejected by some of the most renowned art galleries in Europe was heart breaking. The odds were always against us: it seems the Swiss don't like cameras, or cold callers at galleries.

The last call of the day was particularly awful. We stumbled into a little alternative gallery and Johan was greeted by the owner, who also happened to be a professor at the town's art academy. He proceeded to give a less than favourable critique of his portrait work, on camera. I have absolute respect for Johan for the way he took this. Not least because art is subjective and this man's view, while trained, was a) not requested and b) not necessarily correct (there are plenty of serious art collectors who own Johan's work for example, who would definitely disagree, as do I).

Physically exhausted, Johan discovers a ten-euro note buried in the murky depths of his rucksack, which the producer, in a moment of compassion, offers to change at a favourable exchange rate into Swiss currency. Zurich is expensive, ludicrously expensive; it won't get us dinner, but we can survive a few hours on it, hopefully.

The crew (reluctantly, to give them their due) leave us to get themselves dinner. They must have been exhausted too, also carrying heavy equipment and following us continuously.

Left alone, Johan and I decide to make our way back to the area of town we saw on our first arrival, full of bars and cafés. Maybe I can try busking there? But our current state of exhaustion overwhelms us. We both, quite literally, collapse in a street. I have never felt anything like it. Without the possibility of a sale or the camera's presence, any last hint of adenaline has gone. For the first time on the journey I actually felt a little scared. It is one thing to have no money, but this was our health and, at the risk of sounding over dramatic, (and trust me, I am not), I suddenly realised we were in deep trouble.

We couldn't afford dinner, let alone a room for tonight to rest up, and we had absolutely no strength to busk or sketch. We made a decision to get to the nearest place we could sit, which ended up being an Irish bar, where we exchanged our precious Swiss note for one beer. We figured with empty bellies, this would suffice in providing at least enough inebriation to numb us temporarily.

Numb us it did not, but it did seem to give Johan back his amiable, confident air which seldom fails to charm complete strangers. After little more than ten minutes, he had struck up a conversation with the people on the table next to us and before I knew it he had pretty much instigated an international outdoor party. There was the New Zealand girl with her Swiss-German boyfriend who, after hearing of our plight, provided us with a constant supply of beer, the two Swiss French men who went off and came back with noodles from a nearby takeaway for us both, and the German man with his Canadian business associate with whom I had some very important and intense conversation, the subject of which, after several cold ones I absolutely cannot remember.

The noodles had been a late arrival in the proceedings, and we were already completely trashed by the time the producer and crew found us and tried to film. Even in these circumstances (or precisely because of them) the producer was keen to interview us. On observing our state, he told us to enjoy the night and that they would come back and film later, but I was still sharp enough to understand this would make us look ridiculous and opted for a semi-drunk interview there and then, rather than an inevitably incoherent one later. I was shocked but not altogether surprised that he would want to take advantage of our weakened state, but at least he agreed to an early interview.

Later, the crew, minus the producer (who, it transpires, despite his greed for dramatic TV, did feel genuinely awful about our situation), joined us with our new friends at the bar. We had decided at some point shortly after the noodles and with offers of free beer still coming our way, that with absolutely no money and an almost one hundred percent chance of a repeat of last night, we might as well be homeless drunks this time around.

For the first time that day, we were at least entirely successful at one thing – reaching oblivion – and the rest, including our salvation, is now a post-filming blur.

**Thursday 19th August DAY 20
– ZURICH, SWITZERLAND**

I do vaguely remember one of the conversations with the German and Canadian businessmen: at one point, the German, realising our predicament was indeed genuine, offered for us to share his hotel room in the business district. It had twin beds, one for him and one Johan could sleep in, and a separate double sofa bed which I could share with Stef, who was welcome to come too as a female presence to ensure everything was above board.

I don't remember so much about the ensuing covert mission to get us into the hotel, or agreeing to leave everything in the German's car in the car park so as not to alert the night porter to our intentions to stay. I do remember, after a large bottle of water in the room, suddenly sobering up, panicking at not having the cello near me and bursting into tears. Exhaustion, malnutrition, alcohol – not a good combination.

The German, who we had by now discovered was called Torsten, was amazing. He went all the way back down and fetched the cello, so I knew it was safe in the room with me, fed me more water and sorted out the sofa bed for Stef and me. Random kindness did exist in Switzerland; only problem was, it was proffered by a fellow foreigner.

This morning we all left together with promises to meet our saviour later. The producer had called, grateful for Torsten's act of generosity, and said he would buy him dinner from the production budget to say thank you. I had to hand it him, this was a lovely gesture.

Waking up with a hangover on a journey this intense is not a clever or pleasant thing. I'm also pretty sure we didn't get that much sleep last night either. Certainly not enough to make up for the lack thereof the night before. I was so happy to have Stef there with me as we negotiated our way out of the high-rise business district. With no idea of where exactly we were or what to do next, Johan realised he had lost part of the microphone stand out of the back of our tartan granny trolley and insisted, despite his clearly weak state and our protestations, on back-tracking to find it.

Stef and I eventually had to let him go and found a little café where we could sit outside and wait for him. Thankfully the weather had improved; it was sunny and warm despite being early morning.

Waiting for Johan and the rest of the crew to turn up, we talk about last night and my sudden emotional outburst. I tell her I am also a little exhausted at how much I feel I have to mother Johan and be the chief organiser, but that I also acknowledge it is my fault for taking on the role. She surprises me by saying that they have all been aware there is an imbalance and that this must be hard for me.

The crew finally find us and order breakfast, sneaking me bits of leftover bread and water when the producer isn't looking. I sell a CD to a passer-by, which will at least buy a coffee each for me and Johan, who is still worryingly AWOL.

Johan does eventually return, mumbling about gallery leads he had tried and looking shattered. I feel a sudden overwhelming sense of respect for him, he's clearly trying hard to make our situation better somehow, and misguided or not given our current levels of exhaustion I feel guilty for my earlier outburst with Stef. I am still outside the little café; the owners have been fantastic, never trying to move me on and even letting me charge my phone. I give Johan a coffee and some of the leftover bread I have saved for him.

Eventually Johan and the crew decide to go to a nearby park to see if he can get some portrait commissions. I have been ordered to wait here and rest up, and for once I don't feel like disobeying.

I think about our next move. I decide it is probably sensible to try and keep travelling, since we've exhausted all leads here. Basel seems like a sensible strategic choice, not too far, also full of galleries, but we'll need to make the train fare. We don't even really have the option of sleeping rough again as the safest place would be the station and the guards recognise us now. Suddenly this journey really has become all about survival. All that matters is that we earn enough to get to Basel and find somewhere safe to sleep there tonight.

I walk to the park to join the others and find poor Johan exhausted, asleep on the grass with the crew filming him. I suddenly feel very protective towards him and angry about this invasion of his privacy. Given the current circumstances I feel he should be able to enjoy his right to rest without being observed and recorded by a camera – I am sure it would already be very clear to a TV audience that we were tired – and this current attempt at documentation seems trivial and crossing the line into tacky reality TV land.

The producer is talking to a man who has wandered over to see what we are doing. He is around my age. I tell him about the journey and about our current predicament. He surprises me with an offer for us to use his flat for an hour or two, so at least so we can get a shower and a short rest. He lives opposite the park and we can go in in an hour.

I thank him profusely: it's something I would never dream of doing normally but right now I have no strength to be suspicious, and besides, the crew are only a phone call away. We will be there.

Johan woke up shortly after and promptly managed to get a portrait commission from a nearby shop owner to whom I also sold a CD. On average we've sold the CDs for 10€ each, although some people, on hearing about our challenge, have chosen to donate a little extra. But now Johan surpasses any previous sale, returning from a conversation with another passer-by minus one CD and clutching a 100€ note. It turns out our generous sponsor (because, let's face it, she isn't paying market value for the disc) had once taken a similar journey, minus a TV crew, and was so sympathetic she wanted to help and also repay in some way the kindness she had experienced years before on her trip. I am astounded by this act of generosity and hope I might get the chance to do the same at some point in the future. I am also surprised by how quickly our situation changes during this trip. All of a sudden we are able to survive again – and purely thanks to the random kindness of the people around us.

It seems our fortunes are truly improving once more. We head to my park encounter's house, who turns out to be a wonderful Swiss man, named Nick. He tells me over a sandwich and a beer, while Johan is showering, that he was actually born in India and lived there for the first twelve years of his life. This doesn't surprise me. He has a laid back, open, air about him I have not encountered so far in this country. I took a shower, my first in days (it was delicious) and while Johan took a power nap, we continued our conversation and Nick told me about his job as a sports journalist and his proposed sabbatical. I tell him more about our journey and he immediately offers for us to stay. I accept straight away, knowing Johan will gladly agree when he wakes up. I offer a CD and portrait in 'payment' for his offer.

Suddenly it seems that yet again we will be ok. We started the day with nothing and now, thanks to today's encounters and Nick's generosity, we will have enough cash to get us to Basel tomorrow and somewhere to sleep tonight. We meet with the crew, who had chosen not to film us in Nick's flat and are instead entertaining Torsten at the same café that had been my point of refuge for most of the day. He is going home to Germany tomorrow and has offered us accommodation in Stuttgart, where he lives, for this coming weekend. I go to sleep happy and relieved that we have a new plan and guaranteed accommodation this weekend, as long as we make enough money in Basel to get us there. I've done some research on Nick's computer tonight and found out we will need another 140€ to make it there. But after seeing how our fortunes changed today, I feel a renewed sense of optimism, in view of our experience over the past few days, that in life anything is possible.

Nick has gone out and left us the keys for the flat, his home. He has known us fewer than twelve hours. I understand the presence of the TV crew might give us a little more credibility than would normally be afforded to random travellers, but even so this is a big gesture. The TV crew have, in fact, been non-existent since our initial meeting in the park and, following our conversation this afternoon, I'm fairly sure it bears little, if in fact no, relevance to his decision to invite us into his home. Johan and I decide to save our money for the train tomorrow and go to a local supermarket so we can eat dinner cheaply at Nick's. We sit down to our meal of random Swiss delights and grin at each other. I look around Nick's kitchen. The walls are covered in polaroids of different smiling people who I guess are his friends – or missing travellers who all disappeared after meeting a 'nice' Swiss man in a Zurich park.

Friday 20th August DAY 21
– ZURICH – BASEL SWITZERLAND

Johan is asleep in Nick's living room and I am in his little office in my sleeping bag on a mattress, which is surprisingly cosy. On first waking, I had that disturbing feeling of having absolutely no idea where I was. It took me quite a while to process, what with the persisting hangover (it takes a day longer to recover now I am older) or early onset Alzheimer's, but either way Nick's coffee sorts me out. He's already been out and bought fresh bread and yoghurt for us and the stereo is playing 1970s London punk.

We sit and chat some more while Johan gets ready

and I feel a happiness I haven't felt in days. This comes to an abrupt end with the sudden invasion of the TV crew who want to interview Nick.

The producer's line of questioning instantly irritates me: immature jibes at the Swiss. I am embarrassed after how much generosity Nick has shown us. He bravely engages in the interview, despite the quality and pointlessness of the inquisition, and insists on giving us the leftover bread from breakfast and a bottle of white rum he acquired on his previous travels as we finally say goodbye.

Another life with which we had been in brief collision. Another reminder that there are some really decent people in the world.

We plan to walk to the train station and stop a random man for directions. Seeing the amount of luggage we are carrying, he offers to give us a lift. He rearranges the entire contents of his boot to fit all our belongings, just to take us ten minutes up the road. On hearing about our challenge in the car, he also insists on buying one of our *Painting with Music* CDs.

Resolving to buy a Toblerone next time I'm in Heathrow airport as a mark of respect for all our new Swiss friends, Johan and I jump on the train, destination Basel. En route, I sell another CD to the two old ladies sitting next to us. It's a little triumph and I feel a good omen for the day.

I feel the only real hindrance now is the TV crew. If it had been up to me I would have got a good early start, but stops and starts with the interview this morning have meant we won't reach Basel until midday. We need to earn a fair bit if we have any hope of meeting our German host tomorrow. It's already a tough challenge and time is starting to run against us.

It's 2am in Basel, and I don't know where to start describing quite what an incredible day we have had. I'm in a large bedroom belonging to the daughter of a rich Swiss watch dealer. The sheets smell gorgeous, home laundered. The room is a curious mixture of childhood and adolescence, so I'm guessing the daughter is around ten to twelve years old. Furry toys are scattered on shelves below posters of Zac Efron and Lady Gaga; storybooks and Swiss fairytale hardbacks struggle for space between a new hi-fi and instruction manual. I have an ensuite bathroom. I am in heaven.

In contrast, it had been a tense start on arrival in Basel today. The producer wasn't in a good mood as he wasn't happy with our plan for the day. Johan wanted to get rid of the weight of some canvas and we had both agreed last night our best shot of making some money quickly would be to visit more private galleries and hope for a sale. In light of our experience in Zurich it was, to be fair, a risky plan, but I'd researched some places to visit thanks to access to the internet at Nick's, and I could also tell it was important for Johan to leave Switzerland having sold something. If we didn't have any luck I could still spend the evening busking somewhere. Despite the producer's protestations and in light of the fact we weren't being provided with a better alternative, I dug my heels in, insisting we at least be allowed to give it a go. I felt a wave of exhaustion hit me, which I am sure must have been evident in my interview to camera because, yet again, it had only been me having this battle. Johan was still inside the station finishing a portrait commission of a girl he had met on the train. The producer could have waited for us both to be present and I was suspicious about his approach, which definitely had more than a whiff of divide and conquer about it.

We had decided to hire a locker in the station for the day where we could store cases we didn't need but, even so, we were still left with enough baggage to make the walk to the first gallery hot and tiring as we negotiated the steep, cobbled streets that make up Basel town centre. In spite of this and my earlier disagreement with the producer, Johan and I were in good spirits. Basel is a beautiful town and had a buzz about it we had not felt in Zurich.

The first gallery were not interested, but they did suggest somewhere they thought might be worth a try. It was late by the time we made it to the '*Laleh June Gallery*' and in fact it should have been closed but they were still packing away works from a previous show. Glancing at the list of represented artists printed on the door, the producer had made no effort to conceal his pessimism, insisting the gallery was not worth even attempting to sell to. Johan though, bless him, was undeterred. Hovering outside the gallery – I had been too nervous to go in, thinking I might cramp his style – I noticed a smartly dressed man walking past who stopped at the sight of Johan with his canvas laid out, through the gallery window.

It turned out he was a collector who often bought from this gallery. Now I know how this looks, like a big set-up. But I promise it was not. I couldn't believe it myself. He liked the portrait, which was the painting of Stef that Johan had spent the rainy afternoon on a Florence balcony working on, but wanted to live with it in his home for a night and show it to his partner. We didn't have much to lose at this stage (apart from the painting, of course), so Johan agreed. Mr Random Collector would make a decision tomorrow and meet Johan to let him know if he would buy it or not.

Cue stunned silence all round. It was only broken by the wonderfully wacky woman who ran the gallery who, seeing the expression of incredulity on the producer's face, must have been concerned that if the wind changed it might stay that way and decided she ought to engage him in conversation. She offered us all a glass of champagne from a bottle they had been planning to open anyway, to toast the end of the exhibition they were currently working overtime deconstructing.

One of the exhibiting artists, Mark, was also there and gave me a guided tour of the work that was still hanging and about to be packed. I found it really interesting, there was lots of play with reflective materials, and I had a little chuckle to myself as I took this tour, champagne in hand, our *Painting with Music* CD playing on the speakers (at the gallery owner's request), a potential sale within our grasp... At that moment, I truly understood the expression, 'What a difference a day makes.'

Right at the point when I was shoveling in my 100th mouthful of the peanuts which were provided with the champagne, the collector (whose name we learnt is Andy) returned and joined us for a glass of bubbly. Art galleries often have fantastic acoustics, and this one was no exception. Encouraged by the collective improvement in mood and possibly one too many glasses on an empty stomach (the nuts had been an afterthought), I offered to play a little cello concert.

It goes down really well and Andy is sad he can't stay, but he has already accepted a dinner invitation. I am not sure what comes over me but I find myself offering to play at the dinner in exchange for a contribution towards our train journey. I don't expect Andy to take the offer seriously but he does. He thinks I would be a wonderful surprise for the hostess, a dear friend of his. I am given the address and told to be there in an hour.

It is decided Stef will come with me. Johan has been invited to dinner by the exhibiting artist and the gallery owner, so the rest of the crew will go with him. Via a brief stop at the train station to top up the locker fee and change into the smartest outfit I have with me – a bright pink summer dress, crumpled from living at the bottom of my case – we take a taxi to the wide streets of upper class Basel, lined with large white-painted houses. It feels strange to be in this affluent neighbourhood considering our current state of relative poverty. Right now, as a busking musician, and currently without my team-mate, I feel quite out of my depth.

The evening turns out to be a much more intimate affair than I had imagined. Besides Stef and me, there is Andy, the host and hostess, and a Swiss lawyer called Ulrik who has brought his dog Stina, who lives in the apartment opposite. Their home is a beautiful, large, bright apartment, tastefully furnished and, given the current activity in the kitchen, smelling delicious. Despite our surprise arrival, Stef and I are also served a wonderful meal, truly top restaurant quality but with the advantage of also being home-cooked – roast beef and mashed potato, followed by tiramisu so gorgeous I had three helpings, leaving me so full and content it almost rendered me unable to sing. But afterwards, somehow, I did manage to play for the small but perfectly formed crowd.

The music goes down well, but they are more concerned at treating me like a guest than hired entertainment. Fed and watered, I tell them all about our journey. My hosts, Christian and Sandra, offer a bed for the night; their daughter is staying with friends so there is a spare room. I accept and Stef, secure in the knowledge that I am in safe hands, leaves to find the crew and her pre-booked hotel room.

This is the first time during the trip I have been left alone with people we have met and I am relieved it is these people. They are lovely. It turns out Andy is also a watch dealer. I should have guessed from the large Rolex on his wrist. I proudly show them my pink plastic digital gift from Italy which, unsurprisingly, stopped working somewhere between Naples and Rome, but which I wear as a lucky charm and reminder of random kindness. Christian is delighted I am a musician. Music is his passion. I tell him about my own project, the two albums I have made under my stage-name 'Bird'. He instantly finds both on the internet and buys them. We also talk about a shared love of more obscure bands (Curved Air) and not so obscure, until exhaustion finally gets me.

This morning, we had just enough money to get us to Basel and possibly share a hostel room, and nothing extra for furthering our journey or buying food. I still have the half-loaf of bread and tomato in my rucksack which I had been planning to share with Johan for dinner. I wonder how his night is going. I got a text to say not to worry, he has accommodation for the night, but where I have no idea. The unpredictability of this journey is incredible, thrilling, scary, life-affirming.

I have a feeling Andy will buy the painting. He hasn't said so; it's just a gut instinct. Either way, my new Swiss friends have promised to cover our train fare to Germany tomorrow as a wage for my playing, so we will make it to Stuttgart. After our first night in Zurich I didn't expect to feel like this at all, but I'm going to be sad to leave Switzerland. We've ended up meeting some incredible people, rich and poor, all fantastic.

Saturday 21st August DAY 22
– BASEL SWITZERLAND – STUTTGART GERMANY

After only around six hours sleep I am wide awake. Despite the comfort of my surroundings, I am too excited to see what today will bring to enjoy them further. It already looks like it's going to be a beautiful day, sun flooding through the large, paned window in my room. Whatever happens with the painting, we will be able to continue our journey today thanks to last night's dinner recital.

I find my hosts beaming on their balcony waiting to greet me with freshly brewed coffee. Christian wants to show me a DVD of a Finnish opera/hard rock fusion band he loves before we go out for brunch and meet the crew and Johan. *Night Wish* are mad. I've never heard such a crazy musical combination: heavy metal guitar from a hell's angel-looking, long-haired Finnish man, with operatic vocals provided by a formidable creature in a selection of stage outfits I can only presume Bjork's costume designer worked on.

Before we left the house for food, Christian and Sandra handed me a decorated enveloped with 'For our Bird' written on the front. They told me everyone there last night had made a contribution towards our journey. It contained 300€ and 70 Swiss francs. I was speechless.

We met Ulrik (minus Stina the dog) on the way into the centre of town and he joined us for food at the Kunsthalle café where, again spoiled by their generosity, I gratefully feasted on fresh salad – something I hadn't eaten for weeks. Eventually the crew and Johan turned up, and finally Andy, painting rolled under his arm. A tense ten minutes of pleasantries followed, everyone too scared and polite to ask the big question.

Eventually Andy speaks, 'Would 2000€ be acceptable?' Johan and I look at each other, too shocked to even comprehend what emotions we feel. Relief, excitement, happiness? Such an emotional week; such highs and lows. We are saved.

Following fond farewells and promises (which I hope we keep) to stay in touch, we go to the station a little over 2300€ richer. We celebrate en route with a trip to Starbucks for caramel *frappuccinos*, a small but immensely satisfying luxury. We relieve our train locker of our remaining belongings, one canvas lighter. We've spoken to Torsten, who will meet us at the station in Stuttgart with his girlfriend. His friends are having a barbecue this evening which we have been invited to. It has been agreed with the producer and crew that tomorrow will be a day off, now we can afford to take one. We board the train accompanied by a group of drunk young men, all identically dressed as Superman. I wonder what sort of an omen this could possibly be.

Stuttgart, capital of the state of Baden-Württemberg, Germany's sixth largest city and site of the 2006 FIFA World Cup. Home of Mercedes Benz, Porsche and Torsten.

True to his word, he is waiting on the platform for us with his girlfriend, a pretty, slight blonde girl, when our train pulls in. We allow the now completely inebriated superheroes to alight in front of us (I've no idea how they think they are going to save the world in that state) and drag our belongings to Torsten's car. We present the rum Nick gave us in Zurich as a gift for inviting us, and immediately cause mayhem as the cork flicks out of the bottle and rum pours all over the boot of Torsten's pristine German car.

Thankfully we are instantly forgiven and proceed to climb into the newly-anointed bar-on-wheels, heading straight for Torsten's friends' barbecue. And so it happens that four hours after leaving our hosts in Basel, we are in the top floor apartment of a German man we have never met before, clinking bottles of Becks and yelling '*Prost!*'.

I think I am currently witnessing two German Guinness Book of World Record attempts: the first for the number of large Germans it is possible to fit on the world's smallest balcony and the second for the largest amount of sausage meat ever consumed under one roof.

I'm not sure how the whole Guinness Book of Records thing works. I'm guessing you need some sort of official witness, which sadly I'm pretty sure they didn't have. But trust me when I say they deserve both entries in the haloed tome.

After a slightly awkward start, mainly spent trying to attract as little attention to ourselves as possible in the way only people new to a party full of drunken German strangers can, I took in my immediate surroundings and realised the small flat looked like a student apartment. This surprised me. All I really knew about Torsten, thanks to the drunken haze of our last meeting, was that he was some sort of businessman, successful enough for his company to pay for a small hotel suite rather than a single room. I hadn't expected his friends to have posters of Homer Simpson in the toilet and giant glasses on the table filled with fluorescent straws and equally fluorescent alcoholic contents. I was also pleasantly surprised to discover, after a lengthy conversation in the world's narrowest kitchen (World Record people, take note), that Torsten was a fantastically interesting and open-minded person.

After consuming my eighth whole animal and tenth litre of German beer – Johan and I apparently having taken on our own world record attempt – a musical jam was instigated in the sauna, which actually turned out to be an upstairs living room completely paneled with wood. One guy had brought a cajón (a wooden box with a sound hole, played as a drum) another a guitar, another a melodica and I joined in on cello, eventually getting the whole room singing. Now this was TV gold and, like so many moments on this trip, including last night's intimate dinner party recital in Basel (had that really only been yesterday?) there were neither crew nor producer there to witness it. I found this particularly frustrating since it was some of the best I had played during the trip and certainly some of the most honest and intimate exchanges of art for sustenance. It seems odd to be so preoccupied with (for example) catching us asleep but not recording the exchanges on which the premise of the whole show is based.

The evening ended in the typical way when in a new country; learning important swear words. Our teacher was a crazy young German girl who insisted, in spite of my telling her otherwise, that I was in fact Swedish. By 2am I gave up and told her I was from a small village in the north of Sweden where my father worked designing flat-pack furniture but that, strangely for a Swede, I'm not that into meatballs. She seemed calmed by this, or at least enough for me to make an escape through the front door.

It was a great night.

Sunday 22nd August DAY 23
– GÄRTRINGEN, GERMANY

It had been pitch dark when we got back to Torsten's house last night. He had explained he lived on the outskirts of Stuttgart in a village, but I was still shocked by the view that greeted me this morning. I felt like I had been transported back in time, or that I was in one of those medieval village re-enactments where I might find free basket-weaving demos starting next door at half-past each hour and a hog spit-roast lunch for an extra 20 € a head. I half expected Torsten and his girlfriend to come out in full period costume.

The view was also in strange contrast to the inside of Torsten's house, which had a typically young bachelor pad feel to it. Black leather sofas; lots of electrical gadgets, no soap but four choices of shower gel. As at Nick's place in Zurich, Johan had got the living room and I was in Torsten's spare room/office on a sofa bed. Despite it being adequately comfortable, I had woken up early, concerned I might be asked to join in a medieval re-enactment, then remembered, in reality, it had been officially deigned a day off by the producer, and gone back to sleep. More alert on my second awakening, I scanned my new room. One half housed a small gym set-up, including weights and press bench, and the other was his office space, with a shelf holding awards, the largest of which celebrated a group sales target superceded. A poster celebrating his company's involvement in a hardware company was taped to the back of the door.

The thing that had struck me about Torsten the night before was his simultaneous pride in being corporate and enthusiasm towards all things alternative. I am used to one or the other but, in my experience, the combination of the two is rare. I normally encounter a kind of embarrassment and need for self-deprecation from people who work in non-creative industries when they hear what I do for a living.

'No, you don't want to know what my job is about.'
(Actually I do, being creative doesn't mean I am uninterested in what other people do for a living.)

Or

'It's so dull compared to your life,"
(How would you know? You're not living it.)

Or

'I had no choice but to do this – I have no talent.'

But Torsten was entirely different.

I wasn't sure I agreed with his view that it was a good idea to rip down Stuttgart's beautiful old train station and replace it with a highly controversial hi-speed hub (and I noticed on arrival yesterday that the station's walls were covered in protestations from locals also in opposition to the scheme). But I did admire his open-minded approach to encountering humanity. Helping us was a natural part of the process of his life. The disruption was welcomed, it was a learning experience for him. When else might he have direct access to two professional artists in different fields and get the opportunity to learn more?

Johan and I were greeted by Torsten and his girlfriend Julia on the balcony, which had been set up with a breakfast spread any five star hotel buffet would have been proud of (I decided trying to nick anything from this one would be bad manners – and besides, there were no suitable napkins).

Even though it was early, it was hot, and a plan was hatched that after doing some laundry (our last opportunity in Parma had been both pre-our-homeless-night and two countries ago, so I feared we were starting to smell again) we would take a drive to the nearby lake of *Baggersee Epple* and spend the afternoon soaking up the rays. Tonight we could go into town and then we were welcome to spend another night with them to save getting a hotel.

One of the things I am finding so wonderful about this trip is the opportunity to experience a little of other people's lives. I feel privileged to be with these people seeing parts of another country, learning about another culture, in a way I simply would not be able to as a tourist visiting.

The lake was beautiful. Not so much for its aesthetic quality – it was a bit murky, even the resident swans looked a bit unsure about the whole thing – but for its atmosphere. It was obviously the place to be for the locals on a hot summer's day. The banks of the lake were packed with people sitting on rugs and inflatable lilos, some even had little chairs and tables with parasols. Lots of people had brought little temporary barbecues with them and, despite my almost overdosing on sausage yesterday, the air smelt deliciously of grilling meat. Almost everyone was laughing. Away from the cameras, gently tanning with lovely people, I couldn't think of anywhere in the world I would rather be. It was a wonderful feeling.

In the car on the way back to Torsten's, entertainment took a turn for the alternative. He was horrified at my lack of exposure to the German heavy rock scene and proceeded to give me a full immersion by means of his favourite band, *Rammstein*, with a track apparently written about a man who ate his own penis. I decided I would not be eating any more sausage while in Germany.

In the evening we took a train into Stuttgart for a traditional dinner at a beer house, where we treated our kind hosts. The crew and the producer joined us too, looking a little bit the worse for wear. Apparently they also had partied last night, in downtown Stuttgart. On the way back we arranged our tickets for our next destination which, after some advice from Torsten, we decided should be Düsseldorf. We had thought originally about Berlin and, while I dearly wanted to go there, having heard about its thriving art scene and keen to explore it with Johan, it was geographically opposed to the direction we needed to go in. Johan and I were also feeling a lot more cautious since our Zurich experience. Technically, if we were now careful, we could actually make it back to Edinburgh with the money we had.

Back at Torsten's, clothes laundered, bellies full and skin tanned, we talk over a cup of tea about art. He is curious about the term abstraction and asks us to explain.

Johan is instantly animated. He seems a lot more mature than his age as he explains how he sees abstraction as being the manifestation of the heart of the painter. It is fascinating to see him talk in this way. We then end our weekend with a final visual feast (what else do you do after an evening of highbrow conversation about art?). And, after watching the video of the aforementioned Rammstein song, my sausage ban is no longer limited to Germany. It is now lifelong and worldwide, no matter how good they might smell.

Monday 23ʳᵈ August DAY 24 – DÜSSELDORF, GERMANY

Johan and I are halfway through an almost four-hour train journey to Düsseldorf. The crew are driving the 199 miles. The rain has returned but the journey is still pretty, clinging to the River Rhine as we travel north, the countryside dotted with old castles. It feels different now, knowing we have financial security. As always I am in charge of the cash, which I have split between my two bags, nervous now of losing the stash that could get us back to complete the challenge. (Our financial security a point which the producer seems less concerned by this time round in light of the difficult days we had experienced prior to Basel.) Thanks to the computer at Torsten's, I have already found us a cheap hostel where we can stay in Düsseldorf and some potential galleries to visit. Johan and I both want to try some more collaborative work. The producer has suggested he do a portrait of me. It's not an idea I am keen on, but if it allows me to incorporate some musical response, I could be persuaded. We also have a definite gallery contact to visit when we arrive, courtesy of Andy from Basel.

I feel such a sense of relief to be starting the week this way. This time last week we had just arrived in Milan and were not even able to pay for the hotel room we had checked into. I am in no doubt that neither Johan nor I would have quit if things had stayed tough, but it is nice to feel a little less pressure right now.

We finally made it to Düsseldorf but the day continued at a slow pace. Andy's gallery contact was out so we will try to meet her tomorrow. Instead, we went shopping and bought art materials for Johan and made plans for our next collaboration.

We've decided to use some of our money to put on a collaborative show here in Düsseldorf. This time, Johan will respond to my music using the template of a portrait of me he will work on while I am playing. We want to see how the music informs the way he creates the portrait, with a live audience. Tomorrow we will try to find a venue. The 'AO Hostel' I discovered on the net has turned out to be a great find. (We are refusing to spend our money on expensive hotels any more and, to be fair, the producer isn't pressing us to do so after our Zurich experience.) Johan and I have a twin room with a bathroom and there is a bar and pool table downstairs. To be honest, I like it better than any of the posher places we've stayed in on this trip.

This evening I decide to explore the town by myself.

I take a tram downtown and walk along the riverside. Düsseldorf is much prettier than I had imagined. I thought it would be a grey industrial town but, while there are elements of this, mainly due to bad '50s architecture (the new buildings were a necessity after strategic bombing by the RAF during World War II), the old town and riverside are quite beautiful.

But none of this helps to ease the growing sense of anxiety I am unexpectedly beginning to feel. I wonder if, in part, this might be to do with the fact we are nearing the end of the trip. We still have a way to go, but Düsseldorf is a northern European city, and it feels a lot more like Britain than any of the other places we have been. Familiar architecture, shop names and the change in climate are all reminders of the proximity of home, and the imminent conclusion to this adventure suddenly makes me feel very alone.

I take a seat at a café over-looking the river and order a sandwich for dinner. I think about the email I received today, offering me the possibility of a concert in the Middle East this coming autumn. It reminds me that I have no idea what I will do when I get back. The only certainty is that only pieces of the life I had before still remain. Large chunks, such as my home and boyfriend, are gone.

I decide to head back and find Johan. I can't change the past or predict the future so I will try and live in the moment. I realise I may *feel* alone but, unlike many people in the world, I am not alone; I am lucky.

Tuesday 24th August DAY 25
– DÜSSELDORF, GERMANY

Today started well. We managed to meet with Andy's contact at the Düsseldorf Gallery and, while she wasn't interested in buying Johan's work, she was interested in our collaborative ideas and offered us her gallery as a venue for the show. I liked her instantly. A little over middle-aged, smartly dressed, she was abrupt and spoke her mind but, unlike the often confusing experience I felt I was having making TV she was easy to understand; a straight-talking no-nonsense chick. It was refreshing.

Johan spent the afternoon working on his portrait of me from a photograph we had taken in the hostel room. I'd found the process excruciating, as I massively dislike having my picture taken – which had been part of the reason why I'd been reluctant to have a portrait made to start with. Meanwhile, I went back to the hostel to use the computer and design flyers to promote our art 'happening'. And early in the evening, after finding a cheap place to photocopy them, Johan and I took to the streets promoting. It is funny how, despite the fact we are here because we are 'artists', I actually feel I am spending the minority of the time fulfilling this role, instead needing to default to different roles in order to survive. One day researcher and travel agent, the next event promoter. Sadly, I feel the one thing I am not doing enough of is playing the cello...

Johan proves to be a much more successful promoter than me; he really has a talent in the way in which he is able to approach and engage people. Earlier today, while waiting for him outside an art materials shop near our little gallery, where he was stocking up on more oil paints and canvas, I met a man on his bicycle who was also about to do some shopping there. We started talking and it turned out he was also an artist. I explained our challenge and how we aimed to put on a show but needed to find ways to promote it. He suggested going to the larger art museums to see if we could leave flyers or even tap into their large database of visitors and contacts. So now, later on, we find ourselves inside one of the biggest in town, where we manage to meet the director, Ms Ackermann. She is an amazing woman, warm and open, and she agrees to send a message to the people on her database, despite the late notice, inviting them to our little show tomorrow.

We have dinner with the crew in the evening and talk about the possible ways in which appearing on this show might change our lives. I realise how woefully under-prepared I am for the consequences of appearing on a television show. I remind myself that *Art of Survival* is for Sky Arts, a subscription channel. It is not viewed by millions. But I still have some fear. In times when the world seems to crave fame, I am aware that I do not.

In my life as a session musician I have met quite a few 'celebrities'. I've even been asked out by a few (no, I'm not going to tell you their names). And success as an artist can be great, allowing you a larger audience with whom to share your creativity and the financial freedom to explore artistically things you were not previously able. But success normally comes, at least in my business, along to the party with its friend fame. And fame is the sort of friend you really need to keep an eye on, because before you know it he's completely out of control, destroying all the things you previously held dear.

I know I have put myself in a situation where a mild degree of fame may be an outcome as we have little control over how much the show is repeated or whether it is sold on to a larger channel. The producer explains it is unlikely but is a possibility. Of course, none of this would do my career any harm, but I'm still not prepared for a future where I might be recognised in the street. It was what I loved about being a session musician – I could enjoy the pros of the entertainment industry but retain my anonymity. And even as a recording artist playing my own concerts I could still enjoy my private life. But what will happen once I have been on this television show?

All I know for certain is that it's now too late to worry about it. Even if I ran panicking back to the UK too much has already been filmed: it will be aired and I will be on it. At least I know a great little village in Corfu where I can go to hide – but then again, you know about that one too.

Wednesday 25th August DAY 26 – DÜSSELDORF, GERMANY

We started today as we ended yesterday, promoting this evening's show with flyers. And we were being filmed, so

I was even more embarrassed than I normally would be.

We found out there is a mini-festival taking place in the same little district as the gallery this evening and we are hoping to pick up some of its passing trade. Johan continues base work for the portrait and I go off in search of nibbles and wine for the show (no art gallery happening would be complete without consumable bribes to get the punters through the door).

I never saw the conflict between the TV programme and the artistic agenda as clearly as I did at the show this evening. While I spent a blissful few hours playing with the loop unit, a steady (small but perfectly formed) flow of curious passers-by popping in, the producer and crew looked distinctly depressed, bordering on suicidal. This was not the stuff of exciting television. It should have been me being frustrated. Johan found the collaboration difficult and instead went at his own pace and defaulted to doing portraits for cash. But I understand it is a new challenge for him and the large oil portrait of me (abandoned partially finished for this evening) while I feel bears little real life resemblance, definitely catches my soul in the eyes and that is what Johan is brilliant at.

This, to me, is the art of survival: tonight we made more than we spent on flyers and food. We managed to go to a foreign town and put on an event in forty-eight hours. We are truly surviving by our art. I am proud of us, but the TV crew's black mood does get me down. And I realise too late that I'm a bit tipsy for the end of night interview and feel upset that people watching the show may not understand it is the making of television that makes me miserable and not surviving by my art, or any other aspect of the challenge. Nevertheless, on eventually returning to our hostel, Johan and I decide to celebrate our night's relative success with a game of pool. ·

Thursday 26th August DAY 27
– DÜSSELDORF, GERMANY

At some point last night, in the depths of his obvious depression, the producer started to suggest ideas for how we could 'make better television' for him. I have given up reminding him we are on a challenge called 'art of survival'. He suggested we should think about trading our art for something. We could head towards the city of Antwerp in Belgium (not geographically a bad idea, tactically speaking) and trade a concert or a painting for a diamond. The diamond trade in Antwerp is one of its economic mainstays. It houses four diamond bourses as well as the International Gemological Institute and the Antwerp World Diamond Centre, the successor to the Hoge Raad Voor Diamant, which plays an important role in setting stands and regulating professional ethics regarding diamond trading.

These facts notwithstanding, I still felt uneasy about connecting our art with a trade I knew had a dark side beneath its glittering façade. While most diamonds are mined legally, a small percentage are still sourced in areas of conflict. Defined by the United Nations as 'diamonds that originate from areas controlled by forces or factions opposed to legitimate and internationally recognised governments', the trade of blood diamonds came to worldwide attention in the 1990s due to the brutal conflict in Sierra Leone, and I had no wish to associate the value of what we produced as artists with this industry. Furthermore, apart from helping to augment our running total, which will be a factor in us winning or losing the competition (which anyhow held no motivation for me), I could see absolutely no point in us being in possession of a diamond.

I realise I have a problem though: the producer's desperation to create good television is increasing. I have to find a solution, a compromise between retaining our artistic integrity and also giving the producer something to work with. It is so funny to be supposedly recording 'reality' but having to contrive situations to be 'realistically' filmed. Contradictions noted, the fact remained that the true reality was I needed an idea, and fast.

Today doesn't start well. I am hungover from the consumption of too much budget wine at our show and a bit sleep-deprived on only five and a half hours. Entirely my own fault. We check out of the coolest hostel ever and go to meet the crew at a café near the gallery.

The atmosphere was tense. Conversation, which was generally non-existent, eventually opened with a discussion on what we would do today. Obviously we should keep travelling, seeking out new adventure, but our funds meant we didn't have to risk anything. We weren't hungry or homeless, and clearly not helping the pursuit for entertaining TV. Although we had all inevitably bonded as a consequence of our sharing this adventure, I could tell the crew's alliance fell firmly on the side of the producer. I understand this, they are paid to make television; their agenda is different to mine and Johan's as contributors. I also think I am easier on them than the producer. It is almost as if, as the creator of the show, I see the producer as an artist of sorts and therefore take his comments more personally. I realise this is both an unconsciously paid compliment to him but also at the same time a little unfair to him. He has not been asked to be recognised and consequently judged by me in this way.

Johan escaped to the gallery to put the finishing touches to the portrait of me, and was greeted by the gallery owner who offered for us to stay the night with her. The producer was horrified at the idea, seeing no potential for entertainment, and threatened to pull the show and send us home if we accepted. A surprisingly emotionally charged threat – despite our horns often locking I hadn't seen this coming. However I wasn't one hundred percent convinced this statement wasn't a little theatrical and more bluff than serious stuff. In reality, with the amount of money being spent on this show and the fact we were more than halfway through, I seriously doubted he would actually pull the plug on everything. But I was starting to sympathise with him. I also had no desire to coast the rest of our trip just because we were safe financially.

I remembered something we had vaguely discussed the other day about sailing on the Rhine and suggested that could be our challenge. At this point I'm really feeling the pressure to come up with a legitimate way to further our journey. Travelling by boat, if we find one, we could swap our art in some way for our river passage. Everyone liked the idea; a collective sigh of relief.

A trip to the tourist office in the centre of town reveals three options. The first is the tour boats, which sail up and down this part of the Rhine, leaving from the riverside. We go and check it out, but it becomes clear this will not be much help in furthering our journey – even though the lovely lady at the ticket hut offers us a free tour, the boats do round trips and do not travel far up the river.

Our second option is the Düsseldorf-Hafen. An area once thriving with industry trade, this came to an end when the Mannesmann company discontinued its tube production in Düsseldorf and the harbour lost its main reason for being. But in recent years it has been the subject of major redevelopment, notably with the addition of three buildings by the architect Frank Gehry, attracting residents, bars, restaurants and a private harbour.

We head there and meet a couple of suitably intrepid sailors in the forms of a middle-aged German man and his wife, who are happy for us to join them on their journey from Düsseldorf. Only one problem – they are heading south on the Rhine to Munich, not much help to us needing to travel northwards. The cameras then attract unwanted attention from a formidable elderly woman who turns out to be the local harbour master. We haven't asked permission to be there and are asked to leave straight away.

This brought us to our third and final option: the industrial harbour where the container ships still work and depart from. It's a long shot and nobody really expects us to be able to get a lift on a container ship, but I am fired up today and will not allow any negativity to hamper our mission, no matter how ridiculous. I can tell the producer is grateful I am giving this a go.

We decide a cab is the only way to find the shipyard and split from the crew who agree to join us there. Our cab driver, Leo, turns out to be quite a character. He didn't see the TV crew, so we tell him about our challenge. Thankfully his English is brilliant and he tells us he will try to help. He's also passionate about travel, and when he's not driving crazy foreign artists to find container ships, he runs an internet company selling holidays to Kenya. I am always fascinated by this side of people. You see one view but there is often another equally or even more interesting one hiding below the surface.

When we eventually reach our destination, which turns out to be a complicated maze of container storage-yards and worryingly little evidence of any actual ships, Leo proves to be a massive help. The crew are lost. We are supposed to wait for them before doing anything so they can film us, but time is not on our side. It's already late, and it has become clear no-one at the office speaks English. But Leo transforms into translator extraordinaire and explains our challenge to the staff with enthusiasm. And, to my absolute amazement, there is one ship leaving this evening, heading to Rotterdam. It's perfect. But it's a very unusual request – they will have to contact the captain and ask him what he thinks.

The crew finally find us around the same time that Captain Jan does. He is clearly amused by our request to hitch a lift on his ship in exchange for a concert onboard or a portrait or both. He is also clearly a serious and professional man in charge of a large ship and expensive cargo. But just when we think he will say no, he smiles and agrees. He tells us that while the journey is less than 200 miles it will take an estimated fifteen hours; the ship will have an almost full cargo and travels slowly. We tell him that's fine, we're not in a hurry, but we also suddenly realise that we're not prepared – we have no food or drink with us and I've no idea what facilities there are onboard a cargo ship. I'm thankful yet again to have the sleeping bag with me. And anyway, it can't be any worse than Zurich train station.

We needn't have been concerned. Captain Jan agrees for the TV crew to come onboard and film the adventure with Johan and me, leaving Stef to drive the crew car to Rotterdam alone. We follow him through the dockyard and are greeted by the biggest cargo ship I have ever seen (ok, the only one I've seen up close, but trust me, it is massive). He tells us that loading the ship will take some time and we are welcome to climb aboard, get settled in and watch the loading process.

From the outside the cargo ship looks just as you might expect, but through the small metal entrance door we were greeted by a fully functioning, normal house. It was incredible, like the scene from *You Only*

Live Twice where Sean Connery discovers the Japanese volcano is actually hollow and is in fact concealing a secret rocket base. Jan explains that these ships are actually built for the crew and their families to live on. The children are literally brought up on the boats. Downstairs we are shown the family living room, complete with state of the art kitchen, bathrooms and children's and parent's bedrooms. The walls are papered and the floors covered in thick plush carpet. The sofas are wide and comfy and covered in plump cushions. Jan has three crew members with him, two Dutch and one from the Czech Republic, who give us a tour of the rest of the ship. The engine room is enormous and spotlessly clean and the bridge, with the help of hydraulics, moves up and down to negotiate low bridges and to allow for the bridge to be adjusted according to how many containers are loaded on the front of the vessel. Jan explains the ship can take 5,186 tons and will travel between ten and fourteen kilometres per hour, but can reach the giddy speed of twenty-two kilometres per hour.

The ship's crew, seeing we have boarded woefully unprepared for a long voyage, share their bread, butter, chocolate spread and milk with us, an extremely kind gesture considering we are already travelling for free, and we eat watching the amazing ballet which is the loading of the cargo. It strikes me as incredible that such heavy objects are loaded with cranes in so graceful a manner, so gently and slowly. It's an amazing sight. Loading takes a lot longer than they anticipated but finally, around one in the morning, we say goodbye to Düsseldorf, which curiously has been twinned with Reading since 1947, a fact which neither town let on until 1988. (I completely understand. With no disrespect to its inhabitants, I too would be embarrassed to be twinned with Reading.) Smoothly and almost soundlessly, we sail past the riverside where I had sat alone just two days before and I have a sudden rush of pride at overcoming my anxiety and being here now.

Eventually, despite us all being stupidly excited about being in this unexpected and slightly surreal situation, we are exhausted and retire to the family living room, where we are allowed to sleep for the night. I am given the floor in the adjoining children's bedroom, the boys all deciding I deserve the privacy, and I am thankful for the gesture. The hum of the engines lulls me into a deep sleep.

Friday 27th August DAY 28
– Somewhere on the Rhine, GERMANY

I am sitting on the bridge of the cargo ship, which is called 'Jura'. The ship's crew are chatting and listening to The Carpenters on the stereo. Captain Jan, who I'm guessing to be in his fifties, has just offered to make us macaroni cheese for lunch, which we gratefully accept. Jan has a real warmth and kindness about him. He is thin and wiry and very alert, he reminds me of a cheeky terrier. After lunch I've offered to play cello for the crew as a token gesture of exchange for our passage. After all, Jan is in fact looking after not just Johan and me, but also our TV crew. This morning they had tried to film me asleep in my room but I was too quick for them. It didn't stop them proceeding to film me looking for clothes in my suitcase. Despite this not being the first instance of this sort of intimate filming, the intrusion irritated me hugely. I felt somehow that I deserved a little privacy in exchange for the achievement of managing to negotiate this voyage. I knew though that there were no exchanges of this kind to be made with regard to filming and decided the only way to deal with this was to allow the feeling to pass and enjoy this extraordinary, unexpected part of our journey.

Captain Jan and I are currently alone on the bridge, him steering the ship and me watching the world on the banks of the Rhine go by. It's peaceful and a rare chance to relax. It's already almost 11am and we are delayed from the slow loading of the cargo last night. Jan estimates we will get to Rotterdam around 6pm this evening. I am secretly relieved. I can charge my phone and listen to music. The most important thing is that for one blissful day there will be no pressure on us to 'make good television', as there is simply nothing we can do but slowly travel up the river.

It's also fascinating to get this insight into a way of life I didn't know existed. Jan entertains us with facts as we travel. He explains that we are currently sailing through an area which was once so badly flooded that 200,000 people had to temporarily move out of their homes. He also tells me how storks have just returned to the area, after a twenty-year absence caused by the river being polluted by a fire in Basel.

I start to think that when I look back on this journey I will realise how much I am capable of, after all I managed to get us on this ship, and I wonder with some excitement what our next achievement will be. For the first time I wonder if Johan and I might win this challenge. As I've said, it's not a motivating factor for me, but I think about how the winnings would change my life. Five thousand pounds is not loads of money, but it would allow me some temporary freedom to create my next opportunity. One thing I am sure about, I have no desire to go back to the sort of life I had previously. I know with certainty now that any longing I had for reconciliation with the Ex has gone.

I've been receiving text messages from people we have met on this journey which is immensely pleasing because everything on this trip seems so extraordinary that I almost can't believe the encounters happened in retrospect, and receiving communication from the people we have met is like a happy, playful pinch on the arm – I'm not dreaming, and it would seem the experience they had with me and Johan was also positive enough for them to want to stay in touch. Nicola has split up with Giovanna and Torsten is in another hotel suite in Zurich and thinks of us. I cannot believe that it was exactly four weeks ago today that I flew to Athens. I cannot believe that it was exactly this time one week ago that we woke up in Nick's parkside flat in Zurich, or that in exactly one week from now we should be in Edinburgh preparing for the final show the following day. I try to imagine how that will feel – to be there, to have made it – but I cannot.

I play a small cello recital for Jan and his crew as promised and Johan does a beautiful portrait of Jan, which he loves. As we approach Rotterdam he tells us he will drop us off somewhere more useful than the shipping docks, and that is how it comes about that we make a U-turn on a river in a 3,000 ton cargo ship which neatly drops us off at a riverside lined with houses and bars with the ease of a taxi cab. We watch our 'ride' slowly push up the river again without us and cannot believe what has just happened.

We split from our TV crew to find a hostel I had discovered while doing some research on the boat. It's a long walk, especially with all our gear and, after almost twenty hours of sitting down, we're not as used to the physical pounding as we were in the days before. But eventually we make it to our new home, situated in the architecturally arresting *kubuswoningen* or cubic houses in the Overblaak district. Designed by Piet Blom in 1984, the estate comprises thirty-eight small cubes and two large ones, all attached and tilted at 45-degree angles, and resting on a hexagon-shaped pylon. Most are private residencies but one part has been taken by the hostel. Sadly for our friends in Düsseldorf, even without a communal pool table, on entering our twin room at the top of the angled cube we quickly decide this wins the coolest-hostel-ever award.

In fact, Rotterdam turns out to be pretty cool in general. Johan and I take the chance to leave all our gear in the room and explore the town, and end up crashing a contemporary art gallery private view. It's inspiring stuff – urban street scenes so beautifully painted they remind me of old masters – modern day Caravaggios replacing the sumptuous fabrics with hoodies and landscapes with representations of graffitied walls, and it's wonderful to see Johan enjoying himself again. DJs play and we're treated to an impromptu body popping and robotic dance show. I feel like I've been transported back in time to an eighties club. It's fun and we only just manage to drag ourselves away in time to meet the crew for dinner in a small and suitably funky restaurant nearby.

I sense the dynamic has changed again. We feel like a collective again now, all the frustrations of Düsseldorf forgotten. A plan has been hatched to see if I can try and play a concert in the famous Feyenoord football stadium, seeing as the team just happen to be having a home game here this Sunday. I like this idea and anything feels possible after the cargo ship experience. I get a text from my best friend, Nicky, in London. She is going to come to the final show in Edinburgh next week. Suddenly, finishing the journey, completing the challenge, feels real and I am touched that she will make this effort, to travel that far from her home in London to be part of our final show. It makes me even more determined to finish this.

Saturday 28ᵗʰ August DAY 29
– ROTTERDAM, HOLLAND

Exactly this time next week we will be on the last day

of this challenge. The 'journey' will be over. I wake up thinking about this, torn between two emotions. The first being, 'I can't wait to finish this', because I want to know I made it. I can almost hear myself saying, 'I did it, we did it, two strangers, we became team-mates and, using only our art as our currency, travelled across Europe'. But the second feeling creeping up on me is an incredible sense of sadness that the journey will be over. I am sure there will be all the usual promises to 'stay in touch' with Johan and the crew (and certainly it's easier these days with Facebook, Twitter and email), but I wonder whether, back in our real lives, we will really do this. As people this trip has provided us with a unique chance to create and be part of a dynamic which would not normally occur. We are not travellers meeting on the road, nor do we all have the same agenda while taking the journey. But the nature of the trip is such that we have formed a close bond, placing trust in each other in various extraordinary ways. The crew must follow us wherever we choose to go; the producer has to trust we are strong enough to take this challenge and see it through (otherwise he has no product); and, most importantly, Johan and I have had to place an enormous amount of trust in each other to become a team despite being total strangers, and to make that work in frequently trying circumstances.

I took advantage of the hostel's internet facilities this morning. We can plan a little ahead now. We've decided to leave Rotterdam on Monday, giving us enough time for the weekend's Feyenoord challenge. Then we will have a day off from filming in Amsterdam. I'm really happy about this, as early on in the trip the camera-man and sound-man had both talked about how much they wanted to go to Amsterdam and it's nice to know we'll manage to get them there for a rest.

I've also booked accommodation in Edinburgh. A tactical move, as I guess it will be busy with the festival ending the same weekend, and we could come unstuck if we had to find money for an expensive hotel. It's not easy to book without a credit card to give a deposit, but I manage to sweet talk a hostel into holding a room for us.

I also take a few minutes to do some much-needed football team research. As is not unusual for a) a lot of girls and b) almost all musicians I know, my knowledge of football is confined to a vague idea about the offside rule and knowing the man who does the Walkers crisps adverts used to be pretty ok at kicking a ball across a field – oh, and I once met Ally McCoist. I'd love to be less demographically typical about this but, I'm afraid, when it comes to football, I'm definitely no expert.

Lucky for me the internet is a veritable cyber fountain of sporting knowledge, and I learn that Feyenoord is, in fact, one of the top three Dutch teams, the others being Ajax (I thought that was a toilet cleaning product) and PSV (so, that's not a type of plastic clothing cherished by the fetish club scene then?). They've won lots of trophies over the years, but are currently having a 'dry spell'. Apparently, as football fans go, at this club they're also quite a musical bunch in the stands. They've had an unofficial hymn since 1961 called *Hand in Hand* (I wonder if this could be the cause of the dry spell, surely they're meant to be running about individually, kicking the ball towards the goal, not holding hands?) and they sing the Gloria Gaynor hit *I Will Survive* whenever they score a goal (again, I'm not sure about this, isn't the first line: 'First I was afraid, I was petrified'? Not exactly fighting talk...). I stop short of researching the offside rule, a luxury I deem we cannot afford on pay-as-you-go internet, in favour of seeing it in action at the training ground.

Unsurprisingly, I've never been to a football training ground before. But, as they are (despite recent form) such a major team, I did assume security would be tight and that it would be impossible to get near them. But, incredibly, it was like walking onto a school playing field. The ground was opposite the main stadium, which was actually pretty impressive. It was surrounded by a small crowd of hardcore fans and journalists, while the team and their manager, a former Feyenoord player himself in their more successful decades, Mario Been, ran around a bit.

The plan was for me to approach the manager after the training session and ask if I could play at the game tomorrow. It was an excruciating wait, but made considerably more pleasant by my encounter with a man called Michael. He told me he liked to come and watch the training, as not only was he a fan of the team but he had trained in the field next door when he was younger. He was a promising sportsman before a car crash left him paralysed at only twenty-three years old. He's now forty and in a mechanical wheelchair. He talks about how it was very hard for him because he had been such a strong young man who had loved travelling, and how he had found it particularly difficult because he could remember what it was like to walk, to be physically fit and able. He told me he was envious of other physically disabled people he knew who were born that way and did not fully understand the possibilities that life as a physically fit person had to offer. He told me he lived alone and had learnt to be mentally strong, that he had to be.

I felt a bit ashamed about all the times on this trip that I had got frustrated over small things; the conflict between my perceived adventure and the producer's seemed a ridiculous thing to be stressed about in light of meeting this man.

I managed to pluck up the courage to speak to Mario Been as he came off the pitch. Unsurprisingly, he was not particularly impressed at being accosted by a TV crew and a random foreigner with a cello and asking to play in the stadium. Europe's once richest team were now plagued with defeats and a young, inexperienced squad. Mario's parting words were that they needed a striker, not a cellist (a little insensitive, as I spied the current striker walking just behind him staring glumly at his boots).

Undeterred, we decide we'll come back before the game tomorrow anyway and try to speak to the press office.

A plan has also been hatched for Johan to try and auction the portrait of me. We don't have a planned location or any real knowledge of how to go about this, but in light of it being a legitimate way for us to continue on our quest to find the 'value of our art' we speak on the phone to an auction consultant I found on the internet who, it turns out, is a little eccentric to say the least. We decide the only way to try and make this happen in such a short period of time is to get the press involved. We go to Holland's second largest newspaper, which is based in Rotterdam, but are told we need to come back tomorrow by the world's friendliest security guard.

Sunday 29th August DAY 30
– ROTTERDAM, HOLLAND

Despite my knock-back by Mario, we are back at the stadium at 10.30am the next morning to see if we can speak to the press office. We wait in reception and eventually get to meet Gido, who looks more like he should be modelling for Armani than doing press for Feyenoord. He's also incredibly nice and, after a short 'audition' which involves me playing a song while perched precariously with the cello on the reception sofa, he agrees for me to play in the reception building before the match. It's a small triumph. He doesn't think it's a good idea to play in the stadium as the team is on a losing streak and the fans are unhappy, but if they win today I might get a second gig in the players' lounge later on.

A flurry of unexpected activity follows, with the erection of a small stage and lighting rig. I'm in time to start playing just before the fans start to walk through. They seem bemused by my presence and few people stop to listen, but I'm enjoying the opportunity to play again and I am massively grateful to Johan who stands and listens to the whole performance. His portrait of me is propped against the left side of the little stage. The loop unit and amp are behaving themselves for once and, while it may not technically be the gig of my career, I'm relieved to be filmed for once on this trip creating something closer to my usual standard of making music.

As a reward, Gido presents us all with press tickets for the match. And since anything given to us in exchange for our art which has any currency goes towards our final total, I've earned us something today at least.

This is actually not the first time I have been in a football stadium, despite my obvious lack of any knowledge about the sport. When I was a teenager I took a job working in the outside bar at Fulham football club for one season. It was a tough way to earn an illegally poor wage. The bar couldn't have been more badly situated; it was right opposite the river Thames, and the wind sliced through us, freezing cold, as we prepared each weekend for the onslaught of thirsty fans at half-time, pre-pouring pints into plastic cups. Even the slightest spillage of lager froze instantly on your hands. We were given a broom handle to defend ourselves with in case any trouble kicked off, but thankfully I never had to use it. I don't think with the frost-bite I'd have even been able to pick it up, let alone use it to defend myself in any way.

The second time was filming a New Year's Eve television appearance when I worked as a session musician in the Rangers stadium in Scotland.

But this time in Holland, while as cold an experience as Fulham, was fascinating. We were sitting with all the press people who were frantically making notes for reporting the game. There was a little shelf to lean on with a perspex shelter. At half-time there was a little room inside serving free tea and biscuits, where we celebrated Feyenoord's unlikely goal advantage over the opposition. Obviously our over-excited chants, instigated by the camera-man, whose inspired creative lyrics were 'Come on Feyenoord', were working, much to the annoyance and dismay of the journalist nearest us, who we were clearly disturbing with our tune. Bizarrely, we later learned that he was actually English and worked for *The Sun*. It was full-time and Feyenoord had won, 4-0! The atmosphere in the stadium was amazing.

The producer had spied the press conference room on our way to the stand and suggested we crash the post-match conference. The lure of the free sandwiches was enough to convince me and Johan to go in, but I wasn't prepared for the suggestion that I ask Mario a question. But it was too late to back out, the conference room now full, and I can't remember any other point on the journey being this nervous. But buoyed by the celebratory atmosphere, I stuck my hand in the air. To be fair to Mario, he remembered me from yesterday and was incredibly good-humoured. I told him I had played in the reception area pre-match and thought I may have brought them luck – could I be the official Feyenoord cellist? He replied I could play at every match if they kept winning.

It was a light-hearted exchange but the press officers were furious we had gone into the conference without permission. There would be no gig in the players' lounge. I understood their annoyance and, as a parting peace token and to thank them for their earlier generosity, I left them a *Painting with Music* CD. By chance we saw Gido as we were leaving and his mood had mellowed: there were no hard feelings and maybe I could even come back and play for the next match mid-September. Who knows? Maybe I will.

Although it was now late afternoon, there was no time to rest. We had another mission to complete – the producer wanted us to follow up at the newspaper headquarters to see if there was any possibility of running an article on Johan and our proposed art auction.

True to his word, Gerard the security guard was there, but it soon became clear that we wouldn't get to see any journalists. We did, however, get to learn quite a bit about the world's friendliest security guard. He had originally been a printer there but was made redundant. He nearly had his black belt in karate, a fact he proved in a hilarious, friendly five-minute spar with the camera-man who, very ungallantly, used Stef as a human shield at one point when Gerard got a bit overenthusiastic. And in his youth he had been a model and a semi-pro footballer, in fact training with the Feyenoord youth side.

While the crew and Johan massaged their karate wounds outside, Gerard treated me to a 'slide show' of his life in the security booth, showing me family holiday snaps and pictures of his wife and son. I found it a bit weird to be seeing so much of the personal life of someone I didn't know and I felt uncomfortably voyeuristic and unsure of his motivations. He then went on to say how he had aspirations to be a personal bodyguard. He gave me his card, saying that maybe someone like me might require his services. I felt sorry for him as there was a touch of desperation to his offer. It also felt incredibly strange to be regarded by this person as being 'famous' and it made me wonder how other people had viewed us during this journey. I have become so used to being followed around by a television crew that I don't really notice them any more.

Eventually Gerard lets us go and, exhausted, we do a final interview to camera back at the hostel. I don't feel we make much sense and I am sure at some points Johan definitely doesn't. Tired or nervous, he often sounds confused and I find myself overcompensating for him, not wanting him to come across badly on camera. But when the crew have left, Johan tells me he doesn't feel that the producer gave him the opportunity to speak enough. That I'm always asked the questions and he finds it frustrating. I realise I hadn't thought it through well enough from his perspective, and I feel a bit ashamed at my short-sightedness and resolve to talk less.

We also talk about the day and he tells me how much my music touches him. He says he sees how lost I get in it and that he is frustrated I haven't had much opportunity to have a proper audience or good sound during this trip. As has happened often on this journey with Johan, I am shocked by his sudden sensitivity and humbled to have met him. I feel so lucky to have him as my team-mate. Despite our differences, we have not had a single row during this journey.

A friend of Johan's in London knows a girl based in Edinburgh, called Jo, who he thinks may be able to help us. We don't personally know her at all so, figuring this will be within the competition rules, I give her a call. It takes a while to convince Jo we are genuine (imagine if you got a phone call from a complete stranger saying they were taking this challenge for a TV show), however once she does believe us she gets very excited. She'd love to help us out if, no when, we make it there. I promise to keep her updated on our progress and we look forward to meeting her.

Today's work over, we decide to investigate the hostel bar, and bump into three Spanish men we saw there yesterday. Before this journey, I had had relatively few hostel experiences: three, to be precise.

The first was in Barcelona. While promoting my first album, I had been invited to play at a relatively small, local festival. A small fee to cover transport for my guitarist (Jarv) and me was provided, plus food and accommodation. We knew that due to the festival's financial constraints we would have to share a room, but we weren't prepared for having to share it with 100 or so other little guests of the biting and hopping variety, nor the sounds of distinctly more human biting and hopping from the room next door. The whole situation was made even worse by Jarv's unfortunate succumbing to food poisoning (without wanting to say I told you so, eating prawns that have been sitting in the sun so long they are tanned is probably not a great idea).

The second was a not entirely dissimilar experience in Budapest, minus Jarv or any regurgitated sea life, and the third was a marginally more positive experience in Croatia.

But during this trip I have grown to love the hostel experience. One of the main advantages over hotels (cheap or expensive) is the sense of community you get. Unlike hotel bars, in hostels people actually talk to each other. These are like-minded travellers, fellow adventurers who want to hear about your journey. They wear the scars of travel disasters like medals, 'Ah yeah, that's where we had to escape over a barbed wired fence after straying off the public track by accident... Ah yes, lost that arm from lack of blood circulation cut off by the size of my rucksack... Yeah, got scurvy living off Tuc biscuits in Zurich...'

The three Spaniards turned out to be equally inquisitive, entertaining and friendly. They had come to Holland to have a cycling holiday, but unfortunately due to a) no sense of direction whatsoever b) no previous cycling experience whatsoever and c) no desire whatsoever to be on a bicycle despite their voluntary choice of holiday, it had not been a great success. They had not made it further than a circular trip round Rotterdam, during which time they had failed completely to leave the town, which had been their aim, and then one had acquired a puncture, which gave them the fortuitous excuse to abandon their ill-fated adventure for the far more favourable alternative of staying in the hostel bar drinking beer and eating nuts – which they had now been doing for three days. Surprisingly they were actually pretty lucid, or at least lucid enough for an increasingly inebriated Johan and me to enjoy their company.

News of our adventure quickly spread through the bar and before we knew it we were getting free beer from the hostel bartender, a lovely man from Bosnia. He was also an artist and showed me some incredible charcoal drawings he had done, via the hostel internet. I offered to perform in the bar to repay his generosity. Despite it being a Sunday, thanks to the cold, rainy night, the bar was almost full, and so followed a gig that was easily one of my best on the trip and yet again no camera in sight to record it.

The atmosphere was great. We celebrated with more beer and made many new friends, with whom we've vowed to take all our ensuing life adventures – as long as they're not by bicycle…

Monday 30th August DAY 31
– AMSTERDAM, HOLLAND

This morning we had woken up relatively late, relaxed in the knowledge we did not have to take a long journey today. One tram and roughly an hour by train on the super organised Dutch railway network later, we found ourselves in Amsterdam. It's now 4.47pm and I'm having a coffee in a beautiful little café, considering a hair of the dog. My surroundings remind me of Nick's kitchen in Zurich, with polaroids plastered to the walls, but this place has the unlikely additions of a large glitter ball and several cats. I've left Johan at the hotel we managed to find earlier. It was more expensive than we'd hoped, not having made any money for days now, but we should still have just enough to get us back if we're careful.

Today is a day off, but I've done some research into galleries here for Johan, as he still wants to try and sell the portrait and abstract. But I have a feeling he won't sell here, and that we should make plans to get back to the UK. We are so close now I feel nervous doing anything that might jeopardise us getting back. If we spend too much time here chasing leads which prove to be unhelpful and have to start paying for accommodation and food for an extended period, we could run the risk of not having the fare to get to Edinburgh.

Stef has just texted me and I am delighted. We are planning a girly evening exploring the cafés. I'm delighted she is choosing to spend her evening with me rather than the crew, and feel a different person from the one who exactly a week ago was sitting alone in a café in Düsseldorf. I realise I suddenly feel excited about the future and what may come of this trip. I had always planned to write my third album this year, how might this trip inform that? Will the collaborations with Johan and my new compositions from this journey be contributing factors in the creative process now? I want to start planning and setting out my options for my return, because it's starting to feel like it will not just be a return to the UK and my homeland, but a return to the real me. The girl who had the world in front of her when she was sixteen. I feel like I am getting a second chance. I feel lucky.

Stef turns up with a box of paints and paper and we head into the narrow streets in search of a cosy café. We find one, share a pizza and paint. It's a lovely way to spend an evening and I fall a little bit in love with Amsterdam.

Tuesday 31st August DAY 32
– AMSTERDAM, HOLLAND

We woke in the hotel excited this morning (TV! Shower! Comfy beds!). I knew we had just enough money to get to the UK as long as we didn't have to pay for a hotel again tonight and I didn't want to risk not making it, but the producer had other ideas. We went around galleries trying to sell Johan's portrait of 'me', but with no luck.

We went to Christie's and met the press officer, a warm and friendly (and, I have to admit, particularly cute) guy called Martin. He liked the work and promised to put us in touch with one of the best galleries in town. As we waited for his call-back with more information, we walked to the park behind the *Rijksmuseum*. I noticed a middle-aged woman enjoying lunch at the outdoor café in the centre of the park. She smiled at me and I had an overwhelming sense that we should make contact with her. I suggested to Johan to go and talk to her; thinking that maybe she would like a portrait. Ten minutes later and our accommodation worries for tonight were over.

A Real Journey

In a twist of fate to which I have grown strangely accustomed on this journey, it turned out she lived on the other side of the park. She couldn't afford a portrait, but she had two spare rooms and was happy to put us up for the night if that could help? We accepted gratefully and entered the world of sixty-five-year-old Cara. She lived in a beautiful, unchanged Dutch house behind the museum and had been there for thirty-six years.

She tells me how she had her first child at eighteen and subsequently married at twenty. But sadly she split from her husband just six years ago, after forty years of marriage. I can't imagine how painful it must be to spend that much of your life with someone, to assume you will be with them forever, and then not be. Her children are artists and now also parents. She has two cats. She is incredibly friendly and articulate and, I realise sadly, lonely. I have been given the room downstairs next to the kitchen. It is beautiful; traditionally furnished and airy.

Later, true to his word, Martin from Christie's calls and gives us a contact. I call the number and we get an appointment with the man that evening. We leave Cara with promises not to return late and walk across town to the contemporary gallery of Martin's friend, Rob Malash. The gallery is long and narrow and contains some amazing pieces of work. Turk's and Gilbert and George's all nestle up against each other, carefully bubble-wrapped. He loves our challenge and wants to help. He can't promise anything but thinks he might know collectors who could be interested in Johan's portrait of me. If we leave it with him over night he'll see what he can do. We do this and head back to Cara's in time for a glass of red wine with her.

We tell her all about our adventure so far and she asks a lot of interesting questions. It strikes me again that a lot of the best moments on this trip happen off camera – like meeting Cara, my best gigs (Rotterdam, Stuttgart and Basel) and the cargo ship negotiations.

I realise 'reality TV' does not exist – the two do not fit together. Television is not realistic, and the act of being filmed detracts from reality, distorts it. Cara asks how we think the journey would have been without the television camera. I don't know but I wish I did. I would love to set myself the challenge for a second time one day, without the TV crew.

While we sip the wine out of short little water tumblers (which I discover I like much more than the traditional glasses), Cara tells us it is her sixty-sixth birthday in two days. She has planned a short trip to Venice with her sister. I have an overwhelming desire to stay in touch with this woman and hope I do. She is so trusting and so open.

I'm happy to have my own room tonight; it's been six days now sharing with Johan. We're also having a rare moment of some tension between us. He has become a little aggressive in his desire to dominate interviews now and I find it a little unsettling. But this is not of any particular importance considering the journey we have made together and the rarity of us not getting on. We wouldn't be human if we didn't have the odd moment of tension.

Tomorrow it will be September. We started this

adventure in July. It feels both longer and shorter in a way I cannot quite describe.

Wednesday 1st September DAY 33 – AMSTERDAM, HOLLAND

It's 9.04am and I've been awake for about an hour thinking about how we will almost definitely be back in the UK by this time tomorrow. Today we should try and arrange booking the ferry. I've already checked on the internet and it seems it's no problem in terms of availability, but we still need to reserve accommodation onboard. We have found a route that takes us direct from Amsterdam to Newcastle, and as it's overnight we can split the mileage over two days to stay within the challenge rules of no more than 250 miles a day travel.

Today we will find out if we will make our last sale on central European soil, selling the portrait of me to one of Rob's collectors. Strangely I don't have the same positive feeling I did when we left the last portrait with Andy in Basel, but equally I know that I shouldn't stop believing in good fortune now. I realise how the past five weeks have motivated me and given me the courage to ask for things and accept help, something given my pride for being independent, I am not usually accustomed to doing.

Despite the uncertainty of where we will sleep each night on this journey, I've generally been sleeping better than I had been in my London flat. I can't tell if it's just exhaustion or whether I feel more at peace now. I decide, given the daily ups and downs of this challenge, that it is a little of both. Some days I feel mentally and physically drained and fall zombie-like into repose, others I step into (normally after conquering a bad day) with a renewed energy which buoys me with a sense of positivity and personal growth that sends me to sleep with a little smile (and, according to Johan who so often has to share a room with me, also accompanied by what I can only presume to be 'celebratory' snores). I wonder where I will stay next week when this is over, and what I will do. Should I go back to Copenhagen, practically my second home? Should I set up a little London base for a few days? But I also know that I will spoil the last moments of this experience if I think too much about the future.

Why go back to planning now when everything about this journey has been so spontaneous?

Cara and I continued where we had left off our conversation the night before. She had laid on a lovely breakfast for us, eggs, fresh bread, jam, tea, coffee and, of course, Dutch cheese. As with everyone who has so kindly put us up on this trip, I am overwhelmed by her generosity. I met her handyman who was also a musician and teacher. Eventually the crew turned up, causing the usual amount of chaos, and I bade Cara a warm goodbye. The plan for today is simply to see if one of Rob's contacts wants to buy the painting and to make arrangements for the final leg of our journey to the UK.

After such a nice start with Cara, the rest of the morning descends into something not quite so pleasant.

I get a call from the estate agents who the Ex and I rented our flat from in London. He has not sorted out the things he was supposed to and it's frustrating. And my frustration intensifies as the morning progresses and it becomes evident I am also now Johan's secretary, taking calls from various galleries and museums with whom we had left messages. It's not actually his fault, I'm normally happy to assume responsibility since we are a team and one of us has to, but I do feel a bit like a glorified P.A. right now and not the artist I know I actually am.

We arrange to go back to Rob's gallery but we still have some time to kill. Suggestions only mildly less offensive than the diamond-swapping proposal are bandied about and a cursory attempt is made by Johan to swap a portrait for a Chanel handbag. An attempt I wish I had had the forsight to try and veto, as it had no purpose but to make Johan look silly as he was turned away and he doesn't deserve that.

A much more practical solution was for Johan to swap a portrait for a haircut. We found a hairdresser's on the 'Bond Street' of Amsterdam. It was a small but beautiful place and the South American owner was a lovely guy. As it happened he had some spare time this morning and would love a portrait in exchange for a haircut.

So Johan sat down to his pampering and I, well, I just watched. I felt the crew's and Johan's half murmured suggestions that I should be pampered too were not heartfelt at all and after my earlier secretarial episode I was feeling a bit blue.

But it turns out it was just as well I didn't get a cut

too – Johan had been mildly butchered on the hair front. In fact I am not sure if a Flymo on auto-pilot set on top of his head might not have done a better job. Moral to the story: swanky hairdressing salons don't necessarily make good ones.

We get a call from Rob, who tells us we need to go to the gallery immediately – there is somebody interested in the painting. We shouldn't be surprised by now at these random turns of fortune, but still, this would be extraordinary. We have to walk across town and what was going to be a leisurely stroll now turns into a power walk which, with all the equipment, is no mean feat.

Rob is a really interesting guy. In his twenties he hung out with Andy Warhol. Knowing I am a cellist, he gives me a CD by his 'friend' Philip Glass, one of the twentieth century's leading avant-garde musicians. I am quite a fan and have even see him perform the unabridged live performance *Music in Twelve Parts* back in London at the Barbican. I am impressed and give Rob a copy of my *Painting with Music* CD. I hope he likes it.

We have to wait for the crew, who are taking a ridiculously long time to get to the gallery considering they are driving. They want to be there to film if Johan gets an offer. Strangely, though, as we approach the gallery I sense that luck is not on our side this time. And it isn't. The collector does make an offer but it is so low Johan and I make a joint decision not to accept it. It's a tense moment, as this sale could make or break our chances of winning the competition, but then for me the competition is not what the journey is about and I am more anxious that Johan does not under-sell his art.

Preserving the value of our art is much more important to me than winning the competition.

Stef had arranged ferry tickets for us all. A mad dash from the gallery saw us just in time to jump on the coach to transfer from the city centre to the port. After the dash, however, Johan seemed frustrated and down – in fact, he had seemed a bit out of sorts all day, hardly talking to our host at breakfast (although often in these situations he can be a little shy, which is curiously at odds with the Johan who will approach anyone with the cameras on to flyer them for a concert etc.). I wondered if it was more to do with us coming close to the end of the challenge than anything else.

We reached the ferry port and I saw a sign pointing towards Newcastle. It was real, we would make it back. At least to the UK. I felt an overwhelming feeling of excitement as we boarded the last boat of our adventure, our last long voyage. (The train journey from Newcastle to Edinburgh would be comparatively short.)

I tried to cheer Johan up but it was an impossible task, and I also understood he definitely had the right to a little privacy – something I had been grateful for him often affording me over the past weeks. So I turned my attention to our current mode of transport and home for the night. The boat was actually quite impressive. As seemed weirdly in keeping with the randomness of our trip, we would be leaving Holland on a Danish boat called *The Princess of Norway*. The crossing is fifteen-and-a-half-hours long, setting off at 5.30pm and arriving 9am in Newcastle. This time, our last at sea, in contrast to our maiden joint voyage from Patras to Corfu, we have cabins, sharing with the crew to keep the cost down.

Even though we have a long journey ahead of us, one thing's for sure: we are unlikely to get bored. The ship appears to be a floating palace of entertainment. Things have definitely changed since my earlier childhood memories of ferries with cold tea, soggy sandwiches and a 'seated area'.

There were loads of bars and restaurants as well as numerous activities. My favourite was horse racing, how on earth do they get them onboard? And where do they race them, outside on the deck? Despite my best efforts I couldn't find the horses (we learn later it's a wooden mechanical version...) and also decided against bingo and the casino (I am not a gambling woman).

Johan and I share a sandwich in the café, which is definitely a culinary step up from the ones my eight-year-old belly had stubbornly tried and often failed to digest (they instead enjoyed a sort of rebirth on the outside deck). The crew eventually find us – travelling with the car they checked in separately – and Johan goes for a wander.

The camera-man asks me what I will do when I get back to London and have no-one to look after. He is making a joke, knowing I have mothered Johan a bit on this trip, but it hits a nerve. I am starting to realise I had done a similar thing with my Ex. And now, what would I do? I had no idea.

A suggestion is made that I should try and get a gig on the ship, but I am feeling sensitive after the camera-man's question and also wary of us being made to look stupid, as with this morning's Chanel bag escapade. While I am desperate to play the cello, having not performed for days now, I have no desire to be filmed attempting to be the next Jane McDonald. It would be entirely different if my concert could pay for our travel – then it would be an artistic exchange, part of the challenge. But we have paid for our tickets already and there is nothing to gain. I am also aware this might be my penultimate performance and I do not want it to be a potentially embarrassing collaboration with the onboard entertainment.

The producer doesn't let this one go though. He needs TV gold and I am its chosen victim. Eventually we strike a compromise. Though we are not really hungry, I will try to get us free dinner in the ship's top restaurant in exchange for a cello concert. Curiously the crew doesn't join me and Johan for my attempt to negotiate this, deciding to stay in the other restaurant onboard and have their own dinner and, possibly because of their absence (after all it is a strange request on a passenger ship and the TV crew may have given some validity to the proposal), it doesn't happen. After my attempt at compromise the producer is a little easier on me and doesn't push my playing onboard any further. Johan is also feeling less than motivated. He could try getting some portrait work onboard, but he doesn't want to. Considering my earlier refusal I understand, although of course he would potentially be exchanging for cash rather than food, something we do need, but he absolutely has the right to refuse. In retrospect, I also think it is entirely possible that this practice of busking art onboard might well have been stopped by any of the ship's staff had they spotted him trying.

With neither of us doing anything vaguely artistic with our time onboard and the crew wrapping up for the night, we do the only sensible thing left and head for the ship's bar. The Columbus Club on level eight turns out to be quite an experience as we are in time for the evening's entertainment. Dinner for us will be pints and crisps, since we don't want to spend what little money we have on proper food and risk not being able to afford our train fare to Edinburgh – not now we are so close.

First we are treated to a little comedy. I use this word in its broadest sense, hoping upon hope that the man alone on the stage, with nothing but a microphone for company, has an alternative career to escape to after this particular show in which he has not made a single person laugh. And the place is packed. And most people are fairly drunk. And still there is not even a suppressed giggle. Nothing. I've never seen a comedian 'die' on stage before. The only saving grace for this man was the fact he seemed totally and utterly unaware of his complete inability to amuse a single passenger on the boat.

The entertainment value went up a notch with the departure of the North Sea's most unamusing man (accompanied by bails of tumbleweed) and the arrival of the Abba Tribute Band who, while only having a vague nod at sounding like Abba, did have an impressive dance routine and set of costume changes. Fair play. Just as I am about to whisper 'It's entertainment, Jim, but not as we know it,' Johan decides he's had enough and wants to retire to the cabin.

It's still early so I decide to find somewhere a little

quieter to finish my drink and write a little. I start working on some lyrics for a piece of music I've whistled into my voice recorder on the phone, an addition to a track I started working on back in Copenhagen earlier this year. I've decided on the title *The Riddle* (I often start with a title and work backwards to create a story that will eventually become a song). So far I've managed:

Should've been, could've been easier
Then I heard you say that
You should go, well I don't know
You talk in shades of grey
If it's too bright you'll find the shade to hide from living
life
And all the consequent mistakes you'll never make
Because you
Stay in the middle in between
Safe from the riddle of you and me

Just as I'm getting into the stride of verse two, and wondering exactly who has been the influence for this sudden light-bulb moment of lyrical invention (often the process has a subconscious subject that only comes to light as I get to the end of the writing process), the camera-man and sound-man spot me in my little creative corner. I quickly close my book (I'm always a bit shy about showing lyric work in progress) and accept their invite to join them for a drink. They are in good spirits. We talk about finally making it back to the UK. I still can't believe it is happening. I am still expecting to wake up somewhere in Europe or find we have overslept and are in fact on the return leg back to Amsterdam.

We are entertained by a solo guitarist/singer now who is doing surprisingly good renditions of pop songs old and new. The camera-man wants me to go up and sing with him. I am weirdly touched. The cameras are off, but he tells me he loves my voice and that they haven't heard it enough. So I join the entertainer on stage and he turns out to be a lovely guy who is happy for me duet on a couple of songs. The audience loves it and afterwards a few people come up to our table to pay me compliments. I feel a bit fraudulent; it's a bit unfair to go up when I am a professional singer.

At this point I feel incredibly fortunate. We decide to go to bed or risk creating a hangover that definitely won't help our progress tomorrow. I return to the little 'rum cabin' I am sharing with Johan and Stef happy to have had such a positive end to a tough day.

Thursday 2nd September DAY 34
– NEWCASTLE, UK

I can't believe it; we've made it to the UK! I didn't sleep well last night, which is unusual for me as I normally find boats instantly tranquilising. But it doesn't really come as any surprise – I would be inhuman not to feel nervous and excited at the prospect of making it to our homeland.

We met up with the rest of the our crew on the boat before docking and were taken on a silent mystery tour, the final destination was the ship's bridge. It was completely different to the cargo ship we had travelled on previously, no hydraulics necessary here, just a massive open space which felt like it should be occupied by many more people than the Danish Captain and his two crew. It had a touch of Star Trek about it. The captain is friendly but seems understandably shy to have a camera on his bridge and after a brief hand-shake retreats to the relative safety of the other end of the vast expanse of bridge we are standing on before I can ask where Spock and the rest of the gang are hiding. After shooting an interview with the producer, we spend a hilarious half-an-hour pulling fake pictures across an imaginary screen. We have been told this will be used for the show's opening credits. I imagine we must look like people at an early nineties rave party without the music as we move our hands around trying to visualise the still images and titles which will eventually be added in the editing process.

Johan and I split from the rest of our gang to disembark as foot passengers, and we have a moment of madness as we join the hundreds of others leaving the same way with their luggage. I have never understood why leaving a ferry as a foot passenger is such a shambolic experience. Everyone is slightly lost and hemmed into an area which is not designed for the purpose of disembarkation. Why, with all the room on this ship, don't they have a special area for this? Why, considering the length of the journey and the inevitable amount of luggage passengers will have, is it necessary to disembark via three flights of stairs? Johan and I joined the throng struggling down the abnormally steep and narrow staircases, clinging on to each other and our belongings, and discussed his mood. I told him I was worried, was it something I had done? But he assured me it was not my fault. He told me he was preoccupied with feeling the pressure of the final show. I totally understood what he meant.

We were both aware from the original description of the challenge that the journey would end with a 'final show' in Edinburgh. There, providing both teams made it, we would finally encounter our rivals and compete head to head with a final show in the same location. And the money made on that night would be added to the money we made a) from busking/sales and b) from that deemed as earnings in kind, such as restaurant meals given to us etc. Even though we were drawing so close to the end of our adventure, I still struggled to focus on the competitive element to this challenge and it continued to feel at odds with our experience.

But suddenly the journey was almost over and we both realised we were about to encounter a completely different, equally intense challenge. Furthermore, we're utterly unprepared for this. In one respect, I was pleased about this. To me, it meant we had had the journey we'd wanted, truly surviving from our art and not preoccupied with a money-making competition. But in another I also knew we would have to change our mindset now to finish this challenge. We had to plan a 'show'. We had to get people to come, and neither of us had many friends or contacts this far from London, our mutual base – what if our competitors were from the north of England, or worse, Scotland? But I decided to shelve these concerns for now and told Johan to do likewise. Right now we still had the final leg of our journey to take. Let's see what today would bring.

We left the ferry for the connecting bus to Newcastle Central Station and I had a sudden rush of excitement; a double decker bus! And English number plates and driving on the left – past Boots the chemist and Gregg's bakers, things so inherently part of the world I grew up in. Don't get me wrong, at no point during this trip had I been homesick, but at the same time these things brought on a sense of familiarity, which gave me a feeling of excitement I had not been expecting. To say I was looking forward to going home – considering my current lack of one – would be odd, but the idea of being back on my mother soil with the knowledge of what we have achieved and an ensuing sense of adventure to enrich and inform the unknown, filled me with an unexpected and pleasant rush of adrenalin.

It was an uncharacteristically warm and sunny day. It felt like even the weather seemed to be greeting us. The minute we stepped off the bus we were welcomed by an enterprising man who was giving out vouchers for a free coffee at his café. The crew were also there, waiting to film our first proper steps on home soil. I decided to ask the unlikely entrepreneur if he would give me and Johan a free meal in exchange for me playing cello in his café.

Bill turns out to be a total star. Not only does he agree but, on hearing about our challenge, he also recommends the cheapest place to change our squirreled euros into pounds. That's how I find myself in a pawnbroker next to the café exchanging all the money we had managed to save for our final leg of the journey into £266.66. It will get us to Edinburgh and buy us a bed for tonight: we will make it. But the pawnbroker's real purpose did not escape me. I waited in line in this utterly depressing, soulless building filled with people who were hawking their possessions in lieu of any real money. I thought it was particularly sad that one woman was handing over her family's jewellery so she could take a holiday. I felt spoiled: here I was exchanging the earnings from almost five weeks of travelling all over Europe, gained mainly from the generosity afforded us by people we had never met before. I think about the famous line from Blanche DuBois in *A Streetcar Named Desire*:

'I have always depended on the kindness of strangers'

and resolve, given the need of the people surrounding me in this shop, that rather than continue to receive I would like to be able to repay the kindness I have received in as many ways as possible once this challenge has ended.

After spending a very pleasant half-an-hour sitting outside the café playing cello and being filmed (sadly it didn't bring in any more business but Bill seemed happy anyway), we were fed like kings and allowed to choose anything we wanted from the menu. I decided on a jacket potato with cheese, baked beans and coleslaw, a choice I wouldn't normally make but I wanted something comforting and familiar and, along with a mug (a mug!) of tea, it was one of the most delicious meals I've ever had.

Now I am hugging my second mug of tea (Bill insisted) sitting outside the café in the sunshine waiting for Johan and the crew. Johan knew of a gallery in Newcastle and has gone to find it and assess whether it might be able to help us in any way. Bill has just left with the details of our final show (or the few we have, we know no more than the venue and opening time) and has promised to tweet his five hundred strong fan base. I have a good feeling about today. It has been a good start and I desperately want my team-mate to smile again. I realise how much I miss happy Johan and also selfishly, as a team-mate, how much I still need him in order to finish this challenge. We still have two days to go and we're still being filmed – there's no room for error and no time to relax yet.

I end up joining Johan at the gallery. It is housed in a beautiful old building, an unlikely space in the centre of downtown Newcastle, containing a unexpectedly impressive selection of contemporary art. The proprietors are friendly and extremely helpful. They promise to send a mail-out to help promote our show and lend us their computers so we can send emails and I can write a press release. I spend ages composing it. The closest I have got to writing anything like this before was my music biography. In the end, deciding this is no time for faux modesty, I settle on the following:

"*Internationally signed composer/cellist aka Bird (EMI Publishing) and award-winning painter Johan Andersson (BP National Portrait selected artist/Central St. Martins graduate) have spent the past five weeks travelling from Athens, Greece to Edinburgh, Scotland as part of a filmed challenge for a Sky Arts Television show titled 'Art of Survival'.*

Competing against another artistic duo, unknown to each other until the final show, they carry no money or credit cards and are allowed no help from family or friends. They must travel and survive using only their artistic skills.

Their journey has taken them through the highs of selling paintings on the glamorous island of Capri and performing on live radio in Florence, Italy, and a performance at the top European football stadium of Feyenoord in Rotterdam, Holland, to the lows of living off discarded biscuits on café tabletops in Milan and sleeping rough in Zurich train station, Switzerland.

Travelling however they could, with all their equipment – cello, amp, paints, canvases and personal possessions – they even managed to hitch a ride on a 3,000 ton cargo ship from Düsseldorf, Germany up the Rhine to Rotterdam, Holland.

Successful artists in their respective fields, Janie is known for her experimental looped cello compositions and co-writing work with international pop artists, while Johan is best known for his contemporary portraiture work. The question 'why apply to take part in something like this?' has to be asked and is answered by Janie, 'A once in a life time experience to truly test the value of my art and my ability to survive by its worth was an opportunity too good to pass on.'

There is a competitive element to the challenge. Each time they have sold a painting, been paid for a concert or traded their artistic skills for something, the value has been logged, as it has been for the other artistic duo taking part in the show. At their final destination, both teams are required to put on a final show during which they are also allowed to try and make money, which will count towards their final total. The team whose total final earnings are calculated highest at the end of the show will win the competition.

Both Janie and Johan have a mixed heritage. Thirty-four-year-old Janie is half Irish, half English, while twenty-four-year-old Johan is half Swedish, half Sri Lankan. Both are normally London based. They had never met before the start of the challenge.

They hope that the show in Edinburgh will be a chance to share with one of the most culturally aware cities in the world what they have learnt from each other's art and experiences over the course of their extraordinary journey. They hope to inspire and encourage local artists and musicians to collaborate. They also want to share through their exhibition, the stories of some of the amazing people they met during their adventure, some of whom had very little but shared everything they had."

I have contacted Jo again to let her know that we've

made it to the UK, and she is full of ideas and plans. She has also offered for us to stay with her while we are in Edinburgh, which is amazing. The money we save on accommodation can be used to promote the show. Her enthusiasm is contagious and when the gallery finally gets justifiably bored of us hanging out using all their resources (not to mention the entire crew being there) I am not fazed, but excited to have the excuse of getting on our last mode of transport and travelling by train from Newcastle to Edinburgh.

But at the train station we experience our first true disappointment of the day. Our producer has spoken to the producer of the other team and they have decided not to allow me and Johan to stay with Jo as they are deeming it 'help from a friend', even though neither Johan nor I have ever met her. It is a huge blow and, I think, an incredibly unjust decision. I voice this opinion strongly. It won't change our producer's mind but I am furious, not just about this unfair decision but also for turning the day into another argumentative one. Thank goodness we have the hostel reservation I made last week.

The only upside is that this adversity reunites me and Johan with the joint emotions of frustration and determination to see this through whatever. We buy our tickets to Edinburgh and sit staring at the English, giving way to Scottish, countryside for the first time together.

WE'VE MADE IT!
WE'RE IN EDINBURGH!!!
6.14pm 02/09/10

We arrive at Edinburgh station and both experience the most immense and curious sensation. A huge but to be expected anti-climax mixed with a mutual pride. We look at each other and can't stop laughing. The crew are nowhere to be seen. I find it odd that they chose to take the crew car from Newcastle and leave us to take this poignant last section of the journey by ourselves – surely this is exactly the sort of moment that should be captured for the show?

But our triumphant and happy arrival in Edinburgh seems to be of little consequence to them. The producer does call, though, asking us not to stay in the station too long or, for that matter, anywhere near it. Suddenly we realise two things. One, that our rival team must be near. Two, that we must have got here first if we need to leave the station; they must be on the next train. We both feel delighted that we made it here first, and in a weird way it means more to me than the outcome of the final competition.

We have arranged to meet Jo and walk outside into the sunshine to see a wonderful energy-bound bundle of loveliness frantically waving at us. She whisks us to a nearby downtown bar and insists on buying us beer and crisps while we talk over plans for how to promote our show. We are very grateful for her help.

She tells us she has a contact at the local newspaper she will send my press release to, and that she will try and get flyers printed at her office and organise a little team of volunteers to help us on the final day. We are so grateful, but she also reminds us that it is exciting for her. She never dreamed of being involved with something like this – the TV show, our journey – and she is also incredibly grateful to us. I am again reminded, as with Cara in Amsterdam and the exchange between her giving us shelter and her needing company, that this journey has not just been about receiving kindness, but also about exchanges of experiences between strangers, between us and the wonderful people we have met.

I receive another phone call; the TV crew have arrived and are on their way. They want to interview us both.

We are outside the bar Jo brought us to, in a cobbled backstreet in Edinburgh and are in good spirits. We find out our rivals got to Edinburgh thirty minutes after us, also by train (as we had suspected). It is an incredible thought. That we both set off from Athens five weeks ago with the same set of constraints. That with different journey paths, experiences and talents, we managed to make it 1753.45 miles across Europe to arrive within thirty minutes of each other. If I didn't know it couldn't possibly have been rigged (I made most of the journey route decisions) I would not believe it.

The second thing revealed to us is that they have gone straight to the same hostel I pre-booked. They have not pre-booked but want to stay there. Will we give up our booking? We cannot risk meeting yet, that is planned for tomorrow. Not for the first time on this trip I suspect we are getting treated more harshly than our competitors, since we are travelling with the main producer who came up with the concept for the show. Rules incorporated as part of the challenge such as 'no help from friends' (at what point does someone become a friend?) seem to have shifting boundaries and I think he has consistently chosen a harder line with us, maybe being concerned not to appear to be flaunting the guidelines he set for the programme. But why should we give up our room? We had the foresight to book and we had been told just hours earlier, with no logical reason, that we couldn't stay with Jo. But now we are finally here in Edinburgh, and after our earlier spat, I have neither the strength nor inclination to argue further with the producer. Ok, yes, provided that he could guarantee alternative accommodation, then why not? They agree to book us somewhere else that won't cost us any more – and that's how we end up in the weirdest hostel of the trip.

The good news is the hostel is actually cheaper than the one we had reserved. It leaves us with £70 spare.

The bad news is it's definitely not quite as nice. Negotiating level upon level of concrete staircase is not a problem, unless you have the amount of gear Johan and I have. There is nowhere to eat and the communal bathrooms are hairy, literally. Which is odd because there seems to be little evidence of anyone else staying here. But we only have to stick it out two nights, and now we know what it feels like to sleep rough just for one night, we feel incredibly lucky to even be here.

Jo, as confused as us about why she can't give us a bed for the night, offers at least to feed us, which is apparently deemed to be within the TV show rules. This nonsensical decision sows a seed of suspicion in my head, what have the other team been allowed? I am glad we are at the end of the journey now and not the start, I would have hated the whole five weeks to have been like this, constantly wondering about the other team.

Jo comes to meet us outside the hostel. Her flat is walking distance and we stop at the local Tesco en route. I spend a good five minutes marvelling at all things British – conscious not to say English now we are in beautiful Scotland! – Jaffa Cakes, Dairy Milk, MARMITE!!!!!!! The familiar smells are also surprising me. I didn't realise Tesco had a specific scent until I recognised it the minute I walked in. If you've ever been travelling for more than a couple of weeks you'll probably know what I mean, if you haven't it's probably not worth it just to discover this smell; while not repugnant, it's not impressive enough to inspire a long vacation.

After a lovely home-cooked dinner, Jo lent me her computer and I spent some time designing flyers which she could hopefully print at her office tomorrow. I also emailed the file to myself in case there were any problems. Her boss's initial generosity and enthusiasm for helping us seemed to have waned and we didn't want to get Jo in any trouble.

Eventually, late, we found our way back to the hostel where, contrary to my misgivings, I managed to get a fairly good night's sleep.

Friday 3rd September DAY 35
– EDINBURGH, SCOTLAND

We wake early, our first morning at our final destination. We know we have enough money to sleep here tonight, our last night of the journey. We will never wake in a new place as part of this trip again. We will never have the uncertainty of living off random chance and adventure again, unless we independently instigate it in our 'normal' lives. It's an interesting paradox, though, that maybe the structure provided by the fact we are also making a television show has allowed for the random in our adventure to be truly embraced. And although I have felt the constant conflict between our journey and the making of the programme, maybe it is their co-existence that has actually made such a journey possible?

Johan and I exchange a look from our separate student beds in our small room, daring each other to be the first to brave the world's hairiest shower cubicle. In the winter this hostel reverts back to its primary function as student accommodation. I can't imagine living here. It isn't the standard of living here but more the depression the building inspires. The rooms are small and inadequate in light. I compare it to the accommodation I had as a student, also partly in halls when I went on an Erasmus exchange to the Danmarks Designskole in Copenhagen. They were bright and airy with ensuite bathrooms and a little kitchen, every detail made conducive to the aim of studying. Here I could imagine wanting to escape at every given chance.

I realise how fortunate I have been in so many

aspects of my life. Copenhagen had been my last real adventure before this one. As I mentioned earlier, I had made the decision to study unusually late in life. After enjoying a varied career as a musician I had been on the verge of what society would consider my 'big break'. I had written an album, my first, which thanks to an ambitious and wonderful Icelandic woman, who became my manager, we'd released ourselves in lieu of a recording contract. Thanks to an equally wonderful PR man we'd also managed to get the album reviewed in the UK by almost every major national newspaper and magazine to widespread acclaim. This led to a substantial recording contract offer from a major label in London. But unfortunately, after six months of contractual negotiation with music lawyers and company officials and two weeks before signing my big international recording contract, the head of the label, and my biggest fan there, was made redundant.

Suddenly the dream was over. Nobody wanted to sign and take on the career of the girl championed by the man who had been asked to leave. Disillusioned and, quite frankly, exhausted by the highs and lows of the whole process, my manager, with my absolute blessing, took a job offer promoting the export of Icelandic music internationally and I decided, for the first time in my career, to put my music making on hold. I was aware of my utter disappointment and afraid that if I doggedly pursued my dream with depleted energy resources I might run the risk of eventually hating the thing I treasured and loved most in my life, my music. I already had a foundation qualification in Art, which would allow me to apply for a degree if I wished. I saw it as the only way to regain my former passion. I would stay in a creative field, but give myself more options by becoming better educated. A degree in music wasn't an option; I needed a fresh challenge.

It turned out, as most proactive decisions do, to have been the best choice I could have made. To my utter surprise I was offered a place at the University of the Arts, London, to study design. A three-year full-time degree, where I split my time between Central St. Martins and my main campus, The London College of Communication. During the first year I immersed myself in the study of art, doing the occasional jazz covers concert in conjunction with a part-time job in an architectural school to help fund my course. It was exhausting but satisfying. In the second year, before my final year foray into studying the relationship between art and music, I was offered the chance to apply for the Erasmus scheme, a European exchange scheme where students can apply to take one term of study in a European university of their choice from a given list. Although not directly relevant to my course (BA Hons Surface Design), I had always been curious to study ceramic design and saw this as a chance to enrich my studies with something completely different.

I was also aware that the chances of me getting a place at the Copenhagen-based school were slim. My course was not directly relevant, they are inundated with requests to study there and there is a very limited number of places. But I wrote a proposal and was, to my surprise, accepted.

I had only been to Copenhagen once before, to play a concert with an Icelandic band I had sessioned cello for in a downtown rock venue called Vega. I remembered only two things from this trip, the hotel was in the red light district, and I had actually seen people shooting up on the doorstep, and that it rained a lot.

And so there I was back again, knowing absolutely no-one. But as it turned out I did know someone. A friend of an English friend who was making music in a disused warehouse just out of town. He put me in touch with some musicians and venues. Suddenly the one thing I had been trying to escape became my saviour. I had brought my cello with me and with nothing to lose on the long lonely evenings when I wasn't learning to make ceramics at the college, I gradually immersed myself in the Copenhagen music scene. I found out about an English man working for Danish national radio. He had a well-equipped studio that he never used, thanks to his job. He preferred to have it busy than empty and offered me the nights there to record if I wanted to.

And so I began to write again.

A friend I had met through the acoustic song-writing nights I had started attending regularly in town came down and loved what I was doing and told me he knew someone who ran a cool independent record label in town I should meet. I was extremely reluctant, scarred by my previous encounters with labels and happy with my current balance of studying art by day and writing under my own steam by night, but a free ticket to a Joanna Newsom concert at the same venue I had sessioned in years before, led to a chance meeting with the man from this label, Kenneth, who asked to hear the demos.

I was so sure he wouldn't be interested that I gave him the demo. The following morning I had a new record deal. As you are now probably aware, seeing as you are reading this book, I am not one for giving up on something, so I negotiated that I would take the deal on finishing my degree a year later in London. Then I went home, finished my degree, won a design award, and then returned to my true home of a recording studio to develop my demos into my second album, *Girl and a Cello*. I subsequently returned to Denmark to promote it, began writing with other artists and got signed to EMI publishing.

And I am now about to complete another challenge; another adventure started in the face of adversity which I hope will also have a positive outcome somehow.

The camera-man had thought of the first mission of the day. He had spent the past five weeks observing me and Johan struggling around Europe with our equipment slowly degrading in functionality – at one point even one of the wheels on my cello case had broken making carrying everything even more difficult – and had decided it was time for me to get a new case. Cello cases are extremely, absurdly, nonsensically expensive. To buy a new one would cost around £900. He had originally suggested, back when we were in Amsterdam, that we could try and get a new one in exchange for playing a concert or swapping a painting. We had made a vague attempt to do this in a small music shop with no success, but now we had some spare time, thanks to our early arrival in Edinburgh, and could try again.

Last night, in between flyer-designing for the show at Jo's, I resumed the role of researcher and found a few possible shops to try. This morning I made a call to the first one on the list. I explained the challenge and they agreed to meet us.

Johan and I arranged to meet the crew in the road next to the shop and, after a short interview to camera to explain our mission, we walked up the steps and into the musical treasure trove that was Stringers Music. While we waited to see someone who could help us I took a look around. The old building was crammed with beautiful instruments I ached to play. Wonderful polished cellos and violins crowded next to each other occupying almost every inch of space in the large front room. Behind a closed door in an adjacent smaller room I could hear the sounds of a very accomplished cellist trying out an instrument, strains of Bach floating through the walls. After a short wait a middle-aged woman came to greet us, who turned out to be the proprietor. She also turned out to be a warm and wonderful woman.

A fellow cellist, she was sympathetic to our challenge and clearly disturbed at both the sight of my travel-worn (nay destroyed) case and the state of my cello. During the course of the journey it had got dirty and also lost its sound post which, normally positioned stationary inside the body of the cello, supporting the structure and aiding amplification of sound, was currently rattling around the body like a pair of spare teeth in a bedside jar.

She was more interested in swapping a case for some of Johan's art; she had little need for the concert. She seemed like a smart woman and I guessed she could instantly assess from the state of my instrument that the chances of my playing Bach better than the (embarrassingly young) virtuoso next door were slim. I was relieved.

So the first challenge was to convince her of the value of Johan's work – that it was indeed a fair exchange. She liked the abstract we showed her, the final one from Johan's Corfu abstract trio, but she didn't know enough about art to be sure it was a good exchange. Her biggest concern was whether or not our story was, in fact, genuine. The cameras made her suspicious, what if they were really filming as part of a 'joke' programme, cheating people into exchanges? Luckily for us, after a brief tour of Johan's website on her computer, she was convinced. She offered to swap a second-hand case for the abstract, which I leapt at somewhat selfishly, forgetting to consider the value this would inevitably place on Johan's art. He would not exchange for anything less than a new case. Fair play.

Eventually she agreed, but not before also offering to fix my cello; she couldn't bear to see it in such a state. After ten minutes, a trip to the luthier (fancy title for cello doctor) upstairs to fix the post and a full polish and replacement of the top string later, we were leaving the building with my cello safely inside the most beautiful shiny case I had ever seen and previously only dreamt of owning. There was also the bonus that the value of the case would be added to our final total. Having reached the end of the physical journey, the competitive element now felt relevant to this challenge.

By now we were running late for an important

appointment. We were about to see the venue for the final show for the first time and finally meet our rivals. Johan and I were both overwhelmed with two emotions: nerves and curiosity. We have to take a cab. I am irritated by being forced to pay for this with the last of our funds, every penny of which we sorely need right now to help us put together our final show, but am distracted by the arrival of two text messages on the trusty iPhone (which I couldn't believe I was still in possession of, intact, after such an adventure).

The first was from my best friend. She was preparing to leave and would reach Edinburgh this evening. The second was from my parents, announcing the same. I hadn't really believed they would make it. I felt so happy that they were taking such a big journey for them, to come and see me. In less than twelve hours I would finally get to see faces I knew, people familiar to me before the trip; I was extremely excited. I was aware, however, that Johan did not have the same and was conscious not to make too much of a big deal of it.

Finally the cab arrives at the venue, the Roxy, and I see it is familiar. I had played here years before, sessioning for a London-based glam rock band. We have to hide round a corner so the other team don't see us. We also have to hide the old cello case we still have with us – I don't want the other team to see we have two, realise we've made a successful swap, and risk them trying to do something similar and increasing their total a day before the final show. Suddenly I have the feeling I may have received a little bite from the competitive bug.

The moment arrives. Our crew follow us into the building and we finally meet our fellow competitors, the only other two people in the world right now who have a fairly good idea of what we are feeling, who also, five weeks ago, left behind their familiar surroundings and comforts to take on this challenge. We have no idea how their adventure played out, but we do know they also successfully made it here. Well done, girls.

The one thing I wasn't prepared for was the sight of the twin crew. Obviously they had the same amount of people recording their journey and it was hilarious to see another version of our camera-man carrying an identical camera, another sound-man carrying boxes and a boom mike, another AP, and another producer (female this time).

The first thing that struck me, standing in the stone-walled entrance hall of the venue, was the atmosphere. For all our little trials and tribulations and my frequent clashing with the producer, we were still a relatively happy little family; a tribute to every member of our team. But I could instantly tell that the other crew did not share the same relationship with their artists. They looked tired and, quite frankly, unhappy. Turning my attention to our rivals, I also saw a tension between the two of them which did not exist between me and Johan. I sensed an almost aggressive competitiveness despite the warm smiles, handshakes and hugs which left me a) relieved beyond belief I had landed Johan as my team mate and b) fairly sure that they had been focusing much more on the competition than having an artistic journey in the way Johan and I had.

And so the game begins. The venue has three main rooms and we will all be shown each of them; we must then decide between the four of us which team will get which room. It's obviously been designed in a way to illicit emotional responses, competitiveness and conflict between the two teams. The first room we see is the main hall directly next to the entrance, and has a clear strategic advantage for getting people through the door and into your show. But the room is huge and, to be honest, not really right for me and Johan. The large hall acoustics will not be beneficial for my electronic music and the walls are not really suitable for our planned visual exhibition. I notice the opera singer's eyes light up and curiously they remind me – I fear a little ungraciously, but hey, it's a competition – of a scene in the original *Charlie and the Chocolate Factory* just before Violet Beauregarde, against the advice of Willy Wonka, eats a piece of chewing gum that turns her into a giant blueberry. Trying to banish thoughts of my rival turning purple and swelling to a size that would fill this enormous hall, I am then amazed at her first question: 'Where's the dressing room?' Johan and I exchange a glance and we know we're both thinking the same thing: 'Thank god I travelled with you for five weeks!'

Actually all being said, I've no idea what these girls are really like as people. It's impossible to judge in five minutes – particularly in such curious circumstances with the cameras following us – and I have to admire anyone else who was insane enough to take on this challenge and cheat the TV psychiatrist into letting them on it.

Johan and I seem to have an almost telepathic ability to communicate now and we both seem to have thought of the same tactic – while I am in absolutely no doubt that he doesn't want this room either, we both pretend to be very enthusiastic about it. This way when we let them have it we will appear fantastically gracious. It works. After seeing the second room, a small theatre set up with a stage and chairs on a gradient opposite, it is clearly unsuitable for both teams. However, the third room we instantly fall in love with. It's in the basement next to the bar and the toilet (also a strategic plus, everyone needs to wee at some point). It's smelly and scruffy (but so are Johan and I at this point) with a perfect cubic space and an added stage area, which is good for electronically powered music acoustically, and it also has good wall space to hang Johan's work. We make vague murmurings that it seems nice, not wanting to let on to the other team that this is the room we want.

We are sent away with our respective crews to discuss our preferred choice and then rejoin the other team to negotiate. It proves easy: I take the lead and ask straight out which room they want. They make the choice we expect. Our strategy works and everyone is happy. Maybe this is going to be fun after all.

And so the madness begins. In just over twenty-four hours we will be putting on our final show. We go down to the basement and start planning what will go where. The room is not big, but sizeable enough to appear full without needing too many people (not to be pessimistic, but it's better to have a crowded smaller room than a half-empty hall).

We find out the opera singer's boyfriend is Scottish. It's a blow; they have a massively unfair advantage and I think back to our earlier hostel situation and the invite from Jo that was disallowed. Whichever way I look at it, this doesn't really feel like a fair competition.

Undeterred, we keep planning: taking pictures on the iPhone of the space and negotiating the use of the house engineer for my music, whom the other team will not need as they plan to use the natural acoustics of their room for their classical performances.

It is slightly more difficult for us with our two very different artistic skills – we cannot simply put on a concert like our rivals and we realise this is very late in the day to be trying to devise the content of a show, as well as planning and promoting it. We should have thought more about this earlier, but at the same time I'm glad we didn't. This element of the challenge is so far removed and not at all in keeping with the rest of the journey. For me the challenge should have ended the moment we stepped off the train in Edinburgh and I know Johan, despite being slightly more competitive than me, feels the same way.

I can also feel how stressed out he is at the thought of having to put on his own show. Johan wants to exhibit the paintings he still has, the portrait of me which we didn't sell in Amsterdam plus the huge abstract canvas that inspired my *Painting with Music* CD back in Rome, which we have never seen stretched.

It is decided he will work on finding materials to do this and I will get on with tracking down a printer's and trying to cut a deal with the little money we have so we can print some flyers. Jo hasn't got back to us and we can't risk not having anything to take around town tonight on our planned promotional mission. I also want to try and fill the space with an exhibition of the things we have collected along the way. My old decorated cello case, the granny trolley which, despite the odds, stapled and gaffer-taped around the edges, managed to transport many of our possessions all the way here. I also want to try and print the photos I have taken on my iPhone throughout our journey. Maybe we will be able to exhibit these in our space and perhaps even sell them on the night? We don't want to charge an entrance fee. It is not in keeping with the spirit of our journey and the generosity others showed us that allowed us to get here. We want people at least to get to see and hear the fruits of our journey for free.

We finally make a decision that we will put on a collaborative show, although I can see Johan is a little uneasy about this. He will work on a new abstract piece in response to my loop music, which I will perform on the stage taking up the back half of the room.

We make a list of the things we will need, including lighting, which is particularly important if we are going to hang Johan's work in this dimly lit venue. We are recommended by the venue owner to try a local theatre nearby, who are normally quite generous. We arrive but the cameras cause some offence. I manage to persuade the director to recommend a hire company and one nervous, filmed phone call later I manage to get the man on the other end to believe our story and he agrees to sponsor us by lending a lighting rig. They will deliver it tomorrow morning in time to set up for the show.

One problem down, I leave Johan and the crew in search of materials. Next to an art shop which Johan and I spied earlier in the centre of town, I see a printer's. The girls there turn out to be our Edinburgh angels. I explain our challenge, hoping for a discount, and end up getting a lot more. The printer's, which shall remain nameless for the sake of the girls' jobs, is quiet. They agree to print the flyers for free. Is there anything else I need? How about big printed signs for the venue showing where our room is? Posters to put outside? And why not get all the photos from the iPhone printed too? No payment necessary. Oh, and you must be hungry – have this Coke and donut we bought earlier while you wait.

Astounded, I call the crew and they agree to come down and film (well, at least the girls will have a job until the show is aired, but something tells me they won't be working there by then anyway; they certainly didn't seem too concerned about being filmed). An hour or so later I leave with various sizes and shapes of printed product, the real value of which is calculated and added to our final total.

Johan and I then have to do my least favourite thing before chilling out this evening: we go and hit the town accompanied by the ever-attendant crew and producer, with our freshly-printed flyers. I've told the producer that my parents are arriving later and I'm going to meet them. I am given strict instructions not to let them buy me dinner, which seems almost cruel at this point. We're not 'furthering our journey' by help from friends, we have arrived and my parents will want to do what they do best and look after me. And besides, I'm convinced the opera singer's boyfriend will at least be cooking her dinner in his hometown – what exactly is the difference? Flyering done, at least by the fact that we have no more flyers (whether people decide to turn up is of course another matter entirely, although I have a feeling that yet again Johan's ability to engage with complete strangers may work to our advantage), I leave Johan to spend some time with a friend of his from art college who he has found out is in Edinburgh (and has offered to help us tomorrow) and go to meet my recently arrived parents.

I am experiencing an overwhelming feeling of excitement at the prospect of seeing them. At finally being with people who know me – and whom I know have followed my journey remotely via my iPhone tweets and Facebook picture posts which I have sent occasionally en route. I also know that I am privileged to be experiencing this feeling. I think it is fair to say that most people who have a fairly good relationship with their parents take it for granted. We're easily irritated, sometimes bored by them, and occasionally feel perplexed, but we unconditionally love them. I am no different.

It takes me a while to find them and, when I finally do, it takes a while to explain that they cannot buy me anything, so though I'm starving I order a salad, not wanting to 'eat' into our tiny, show-promoting budget, although I've given Johan money to have some beers with his friend – it's our last night of the challenge and we deserve it.

It is truly amazing to see them. And a little surreal

too, so far away from our normal environment. Seeing them in Edinburgh would be strange at any time, but under these circumstances it is especially weird.

I have a rare moment of speechlessness (well, you've been listening to me ramble on for over two hundred pages now, you know I can talk a bit!). I don't know where to start. So we crowd round the iPhone which contains an intermittent but fairly accurate visual account of the journey and I talk them through it. It's not easy, my mum is fairly visually impaired and the bar we've met in is noisy, but they get the idea.

Dad wants to see what the live music scene in Edinburgh has to offer, so when Johan calls we all decide to meet and head downtown to see what's happening. My dad has always been passionate about music. It is one of the many things I have to thank him for. I remember clearly as a child sitting and him teaching me to harmonise to all his favourite records – The Rolling Stones, Cat Stevens, Gordon Lightfoot, Supertramp, The Moody Blues, Fleetwood Mac, Demis Roussos... Ok, we should stop right there. And while I cannot very well, my Dad whistles like no-one I have ever met before. If you are in a busy supermarket and need to find him it's easy; you just listen for the crazy lone whistler (in fact, since I've never heard anyone else doing this in Tesco, if you are ever in south London and hear whistling, go and say hello to Mr. Price, most likely near the aisle selling Belgian beers or Jacob's Cream Crackers).

Come to think of it, my parents have also always had a bit of a thing for travelling, despite a curious aversion to flying. Within their consequently geographically-limited range we've never been short of an unconventional holiday moment or two.

I remember a basement bar in Holland, doused in dark red light, that we went to once when I five or six. It was much more innocent than it sounds – my parents have a similarly massive aversion to drugs as to flying so no need to call the NSPCC just yet. The 'new' Jackson 5 album was playing, and so impressed was the bar owner by my singing and dancing performance he gave me the cassette tape (for those of you still in possession of the beauty of youth, it was a plastic case with magnetic tape inside which frequently got chewed up in the machine invented to play it but, unlike the ensuing technology, could be fixed by hand with patience and an HB pencil). I still have the tape even though it is all chewed up.

So we found ourselves, plus Johan, in a similarly dimly lit venue in Edinburgh, watching a highly dubious (sorry boys) Scottish covers band. The producer calls, 'It's ok, you can let your parents buy dinner now,' (I can only presume I was right about the opera singer's boyfriend). I was again instantly irritated: we are definitely getting the rougher ride, and of course it's around 10pm now, too late... So we indulge in beer and crisps bought by Dad, who desperately and lovingly wants to provide at least something for us.

We leave my rock and roll parents vaguely tipsy and happy to find their way back to their hotel just in time for my best friend Nicky's arrival. We've known each other for about thirteen years, meeting when I moved into a flatshare in Shepherd's Bush in my early twenties.

She's always been the most incredibly supportive and wonderful friend. She's also an intrepid traveller. Aside from our joint holidays and adventures and her accompanying me on various music tours with my own project Bird (often voluntarily assuming the role of unofficial tour manager extraordinaire), she's also been all over the world backpacking and climbing mountains. I can't think of any friend I would rather have at the end of this adventure than her. She was also the first person I told about my offer to do the show and it was partly due to her encouragement and enthusiasm that I had the strength to get on the plane to Athens and take this challenge.

It's a big day tomorrow, so Johan retires to the hostel, but Nicky and I go for a quick drink before heading back there too. She hasn't booked accommodation in advance so she'll be staying at the 'student Hilton hostel' too.

We catch up briefly and insufficiently. But we have tomorrow, the show and the afterparty, which the TV crew have told us has been arranged. Tomorrow is a big day and I'll need a clear head and a good night's sleep to deal with it.

**Saturday 4th September DAY 36
– EDINBURGH, SCOTLAND**

THE FINAL DAY

It's arrived. Always seems a strange way to describe a day to me, like 'Christmas day, it's arrived!'. It's not a train or a plane, it's a day and, unless you have the misfortune of dying, it was always going to happen – it did not travel to be there. But we did travel to be here, and today marks the end of our journey. I am awake stupidly early to greet the day I have thought so many times during this trip about experiencing.

It is 8.30am.

I am sitting in a little coffee shop near the hostel.

I am having immense difficulty dealing with the emotion I am feeling right now; the one that woke me up and is making me so alert. It's not fear or raw anxiety. I have some excitement, I understand that – we made it, we're here, and it's the last day. Whatever happens now, we completed the challenge. But there are nerves too.

We have a show to put on tonight. There is a competition. We are being filmed. Finally tonight, after six weeks, I will get my purse back. I can almost hear the whoops of joy from my numerous credit card companies, 'She's back!' (I dread to think how my plastic abstinence has affected their end of year bonus). But worry not, money lenders of the world, Janie's back and tonight she intends to make up for it: I can finally treat the crew and Johan to a pint or four.

More friends have announced they are travelling from

their respective south England bases to Edinburgh for the show tonight – my mate Rich from Oxford, Nath and Howard from London. I'm indescribably happy about this. It's massively reassuring to have support from all these people I cherish. Tonight the winners are announced. Tonight we celebrate whatever the outcome.

I start to wonder how I will feel tomorrow. It's a curious thing. No, more than a curious thing. It's a massive thing; to spend five weeks physically and mentally in a place you never expected to be, being filmed almost the entire time, and then that's it, thanks very much. I haven't booked or planned my return from Edinburgh yet. I have no home of my own to go back to. No-one waiting for me. It sounds a bit sad, but I'm not. I left behind the pain of my break-up and the challenge allowed me to escape my loneliness. Now I have a fresh start to look forward to, encouraged by the knowledge that I made it through this. I feel strong.

Whatever happens tonight I can afford to keep travelling for a month or two if I want. I have a new album to plan and make and a world in front of me that few people do. I am incredibly grateful and also proud to have built the life I have for myself. I have learnt not to fear the unknown – and know that if I trust in myself and the people I choose to have around me then the universe will help everything work out in just the way it is meant to be.

Johan, Nicky and I make an early start, getting to the venue as soon as it opens at 10am. I am finding the increasingly competitive nature of this part of the challenge difficult and unsettling. Their posters, our posters, side by side with arrows pointing in opposing directions to our respective performance spaces. Flyers 'going missing' (not a practice Johan and I have indulged in despite some light-hearted encouragement from the producer, who correctly predicted it would happen to us). To be quite honest, I find it all a bit childish, and as a performer this sentiment is fairly alien to me. Working together is what makes great shows. Johan finishes building the frame for his abstract while Nicky and I go in search of materials we need for putting on the show. The pound shop instantly becomes our best friend.

Another curious thing about my parents – which you can verify with them when you meet them in the cracker aisle in Tesco's – is their unashamed addiction to pound shops. And I get why. It is a veritable Aladdin's cave. A treasure trove. The problem is it is almost all trash. It is interesting that in our environmentally conscious day and age a shop producing that much plastic and packaging for no real human use whatsoever can actually be legal.

No matter, as today, for us, all environmentally conscious decisions are suspended in lieu of buying numerous ozone-layer-killing trinkets to decorate our temporary venue. And decorating it will definitely be necessary to transform it from grunge venue into final show material. Though we instantly fell in love with the venue yesterday, I think in part today's nerves about the show are not only to do with its content but also its aesthetic. Unlike our rivals' main hall which was ready made for a classical concert, our room has sticky floors, broken chairs on an old stage and pieces of old black cloth hiding the ravaged walls. Luckily we seem to have quite a little army of helpers. Jo arrived with a friend, Johan's old college mate joined us, and we have Nicky.

We had to take a frustrating early break (we needed all the time we could get) for a 'publicity' photo shoot for Sky Arts. But it was interesting if for no other reason than to demonstrate the massive differences between the two teams. Johan and I came outside in our travelling/ work clothes; our rivals came out in designer evening dresses complete with masks. My cello, despite its polish, was looking as ragged as me and Johan; the other girl's looked like it had come straight out of the Stringers show room I'd been in yesterday. I didn't feel jealous, though. We felt real, the journey had been real, and dressing up would have seemed somehow fake considering what we had been through.

Slowly, Johan, I and our merry and wonderful gang of helpers transform the venue. We decide to hang Johan's paintings prominently on the two walls. The lighting rig arrives and the crew help us set up. It is the first time they have been allowed to do anything for us and I am so heart-warmed to see their enthusiastic and genuine desire to pitch in.

I make an exhibition area in the small room outside ours, which we also have, positioning the cello case, the granny trolley and the bits and pieces we have collected along the way. It's an odd feeling I experience as I prop up my pizza box painting from the Amsterdam bar and a business card from the Greek restaurant we went to that first night, which recommended the hotel of not-so-ill repute. And I start to cover the remaining walls with the hundred or so photos I took on the trip. The night in

Zurich train station, with Johan and the producer asleep on the bench, feels like a very long time ago now.

One by one my other friends arrive in Edinburgh and this helps to ease the nerves, particularly during a stressful moment when we realise the sound guy I negotiated the day before is late. Our TV sound-man is a star though and steps in to help me. It is also a grand gesture because he has been so aware of all the sound problems I have encountered on the trip and he desperately wants me to have at least a good final show. It's really not in his job description and it means a lot to me. And of course, show time comes around ridiculously quickly. Johan and I decide to 'keep it real' dress-wise – and sadly I didn't quite manage to collect enough animal print to win that challenge (though I don't think the producer would have been keen on me being filmed on the final night dressed as an assortment of safari animals anyway).

At 7.30pm our little crew, Jo and her brilliant friend Beth, Steve and Nicky stopped lighting the last candles we had placed around our transformed basement venue and we waited for the people we hoped would turn up. The room quickly became full enough for a concert. I positioned myself on the stage and launched into a loop jam. Johan had pre-prepared a large sheet of canvas on the middle of the venue floor and he finally braved it and started to paint abstraction purely in response to the music. A little girl (who couldn't have been older than two or two-and-a-half) wandered over and started painting with Johan. We had kept the venue fairly chairless to allow people to wander around and look at the photos we had priced up around the wall. This meant that we now had a warm relaxed atmosphere.

People were standing at the back, sitting on the floor, while Johan and his young assistant painted and I played. It was perfect. Screw the competition: we had managed to create a perfect and fitting end to our journey. A new collaborative show, shared by an open-minded and friendly crowd. I genuinely didn't care what happened next or how the classical sit down concert upstairs was going.

An outside bidder bought Johan's painting of me just before the end of our show, my cello case was filled with donations that would go towards our end total and we sold the last of the *Painting with Music* CDs. In every way, for us at least, our final show was a success.

Nine-thirty arrived in what felt like the space of ten minutes (technically, for the more mathematically aware of you, it had been two hours).

And so the last of the madness began. Stef counted our evening's earnings to add to our 'final total' while we had a brief interview to camera. Then we were all moved to the hall upstairs for the 'big announcement'. The two teams were positioned at the front of the hall and both sets of audience combined.

Each team was to choose an envelope containing one of the team's final total. Our beautiful little painting assistant, too young to be aware of the formality of the situation, wandered over, despite the presence of the cameras and audience, and I asked her to pick one. It was ours. I read out the result. The other team's envelope was given to them and thus the final result was revealed.

Now everyone knows a good book (or even a not so

good one) ends on a cliffhanger. Bearing this in mind, I'm not going to tell you the result: you'll have to find out some other way...

But there is still a little more of my experience to recount. Now you've come this far, you should at least celebrate the afterparty with me.

Relief instantly washed over me. The competition was over. The journey complete.

Cars had been arranged to take the crews, the teams and their close family and friends to the five star hotel where we would be having our afterparty and consequently staying. And so we went from Euro Hostel to the Missoni Hotel, where we were greeted like stars. It felt very strange.

The 'wrap' party was held downstairs in the bar, which was a grand and glittering affair compared to almost everything else we had experienced. After a mojito (or maybe it was two), with everyone finally gathered it was interesting again to see the different dynamics between the two crews and teams. It was good to spend some time with the entire group – and we learnt how close we had come to colliding at one point during the trip when both teams ended up at Milan train station at the same time. I find it incredible, we could take any route, any adventure, and yet we still almost met along the way.

Johan and I, the crew and the producer partied and hugged: we had made it. The sensation I had is hard to describe but I will try. It definitely included a pure sense of joy. An unconditional feeling – not attached to winning or losing, having something to gain or something to lose – just a shared feeling of accomplishment and pride among a group of people who five weeks ago were strangers. Whose lives had collided and created an amazing adventure, a shared experience we would never forget, no matter whether we eventually stayed in touch or not.

Though I was given my purse back by Stef in a suitably unceremonious manner, the drinks were free. I wouldn't get to treat the crew tonight (sorry Visa).

Eventually even my parents (who had made me proud with the level of partying they managed to achieve) left the bar and we decided to go to Johan's room to continue partying. The opera singer had left with her boyfriend some time ago (fair play after five weeks away), but the cellist joined our little late-night party. We sunk red wine until the wee hours, swapping stories and generally damaging what few brain cells we had left. In the end we were damaged enough to become collectively incoherent, at which point we all decided to call it a night – or early morning as it almost was.

Sunday 5th September
– EDINBURGH, SCOTLAND
(The fat lady sings.)

Well, it's not over until she does, though in my case it's a kilted bagpipe busker outside the five star Missoni Hotel in the downtown cobble streets of Edinburgh. I am alone, but I can honestly say I feel no anxiety, just happiness. I have had a haircut and bought a new pair of jeans and a jumper. I have lost so much weight nothing I initially packed fits me anymore.

It's a curious sensation, yesterday already feels like a long time ago. I suppose an anti-climax type feeling would be natural but I do not feel any type of depression, just a sense of calm. This morning my hangover and I joined various other hangovers, accompanied by shells of humans (previously known as our crew) for breakfast. This really was the buffet to beat all others so far on the trip; smoked salmon, eggs to order, freshly baked breads in all shapes and sizes...excitement coupled by mild disappointment that I really couldn't justify nicking anything now the challenge was over and I had my purse back.

Too soon it was time for goodbyes. Two of the hotel rooms had been booked for an extra night, so Stef and I had decided to stay so we could catch the famous firework display to mark the end of the Edinburgh Festival, and since I really had nowhere particular to be, then why not? One by one I said goodbye to the rest of the crew, my parents and friends until it was just me, Nicky and Johan. We walked him to the station (I couldn't let him go alone) and, despite our closeness now and a bond and friendship I knew would continue, I also felt it was entirely the right time and way to say goodbye. It was time to take our separate travels, and yet curiously this thought did not make me feel alone, just stronger somehow. Nicky left next – and so it was just me and a day to readjust in Edinburgh.

Sitting outside a café in the centre of town earlier today a man came up to me and asked if I was the girl playing last night for the TV show. I laughed and said yes. It was a strange feeling, I wonder if this is something I will have to get used to when the programme is aired.

Stef's friend had come to join us for the fireworks and we joined the other quarter of a million people there to watch Europe's largest display, a brilliant way to celebrate the end of my journey, though I wished Johan and the rest of the crew were there to see it too. Suddenly I felt very tired and knew that I was ready to face London tomorrow.

Monday 6th September
– LONDON, UK

I woke up surprisingly early. I had some strange, lucid dreams last night – volcanoes erupting and lava flowing through a town I was travelling through. I couldn't escape, and an ex-boyfriend of mine (curiously not the most recent) was there with his family from Iceland. No-one could hear me, we couldn't make the higher ground and disaster was just minutes away. I wonder what Mary might make of this dream on the eve of my returning to my hometown, after five weeks of adventure and challenge. I decide not to dwell on it and think of something positive: the breakfast buffet was beckoning, followed by a short morning's walk before catching the train.

Stef and I had made a tentative plan last night to catch an afternoon train back to London together, but suddenly I just knew it was time to leave and I had an overwhelming need to arrive in London alone, as I had left it, a little over five weeks ago.

I've just passed Newcastle. I will be in London at 3pm. I don't know where I will stay tonight; maybe I will go to my parents' then plan my next move. I can feel the Janie of old creeping around beside me and I don't want her there – I prefer the bubbly confident version of myself I have re-discovered on this trip. I think I will plan a trip away this week, and gather my thoughts.

I am half-an-hour away from King's Cross station now. In thirty minutes I will step on to the streets of my hometown after stepping across so many others over the course of this adventure. I have no idea what the universe is going to throw at me next, but I know that without fear and with positivity I will be able to catch whatever it is and run wherever I need to go with it.

I was reflecting on the challenge with Stef and her friend over dinner last night, and it dawned on me that the toughest part by far had been the conflict between taking the journey as an artist and of being part of a reality television show. The tension between the art of survival and the art of making TV. Despite my frequent acknowledgement of this conflict it still surprised me. I had expected with hindsight for other things to have challenged me more – a stranger as a travelling companion, having no guaranteed income, shelter, or food, not reaching the final destination – and I realise that the only thing that was truly difficult was the one thing that was not part of reality. That was never meant to be.

I step off the train and greet the familiar sights and smells of London. It is raining, the man next to me is swearing to himself and dribbling slightly, two young girls are clutching Caffé Nero cups and giggling. I decide I need a coffee too. I open my purse to pay, put the drink to my lips and make a silent toast to myself and the real journey I know I took.

Acknowledgements

Simon and the team at Beautiful Books, for giving me the opportunity to write this book, for your belief in me, and support, thank you.

Laura, my editor, for prompting some interesting additions to the text with your brilliant questions and comments and for tidying up my grammar! Thank you.

Howard, for taking me seriously, introducing me to my publisher and for being an all round outstanding friend, thank you.

Seb and everyone at Illuminations, James and everyone at Sky Arts, for giving me the chance to participate in the challenge, thank you.

Johan, for being a top team-mate, travelling companion and subsequently dear friend, thank you.

"the Producer", "camera-man" and "sound-man" you know who you are…you wonderful douchebags…and Stef aka Nigel Man…bellisima, thank you.

Mum and Dad, for a naughty night some time in early 1975 and the subsequent years of unconditional love and support you have given me, your daughter. Because of this I have been able to realise so many dreams including this one, thank you.

Alessandro, for suggesting the perfect book title, and for being such a wonderful, warm and brilliant man, thank you.

And finally, to everyone I met on this extraordinary journey, for your kindness and for sharing however briefly, a little of your life with me, thank you.